They Were Giants 2006

They Were Giants 2006

Patrick Yearly

iUniverse, Inc.
New York Lincoln Shanghai

They Were Giants 2006

iUniverse books may be ordered through booksellers or by contacting:

iUniverse
2021 Pine Lake Road, Suite 100
Lincoln, NE 68512
www.iuniverse.com
1-800-Authors (1-800-288-4677)

ISBN-13: 978-0-595-37762-6 (pbk)
ISBN-13: 978-0-595-82136-5 (ebk)
ISBN-10: 0-595-37762-9 (pbk)
ISBN-10: 0-595-82136-7 (ebk)

Printed in the United States of America

Contents

Introduction vii

The Arts 1

Business 16

Education 25

Engineering. 35

Environment. 39

Medicine. 45

Science 56

Social Influence. 72

Sports 87

Technology. 95

Honor Roll 101

Sources 113

Introduction

Each day we walk outside our front door into a stimulating world. The opportunity to live a long and fulfilling life has never been greater. In quiet solitude, many men and women spend their lives creating small steppingstones that lead to a greater good. Their work goes unnoticed to society, but their impact is enormous. We don't see them on television or read about them in the newspaper. They don't appear on the covers of magazines or on the silver screen. We never see them holding a press conference or taking center stage. They come from every arena in life: science, technology, business, medicine, the arts. The list is endless. They go about their work with a dedication that does not attract attention and constant gratification. Their reward is in knowing that they have made a difference.

This book contains the short stories of these anonymous people whose deaths were publicly reported between October 1, 2004 to October 1, 2005. It was not my intention to write a book of obituaries, but a compilation of the achievements of a group of people whose work has benefited many. I consider this book to be used as a source of reference. This, however, is not an obscure group whose passing went unnoticed. Their contributions received acknowledgment from prominent newspapers throughout the world, but they did not make the front page and no one was mourning their loss around the water cooler at the office the next day. Some were well known within the inner circle of their field, but none was a household name. A few may have been well recognized decades ago, but no longer.

I have categorized their efforts into ten categories. Some areas may appeal more to the reader than others and some stories are not as colorful as others. People do not die in a logical fashion. There are categories that contain many more people than others. Perhaps the numbers may be quite different next year. The selection of people whose stories are represented in this book are mine alone and certainly subject to debate. I am not promoting any point of view in support of any cause.

This book is the second in a series of annual installments. Nearly 300 people are represented in the 2006 edition. Ultimately, in the end the focus is not on them, but on a world that benefits immeasurably from their work. Without their resolve we are all much poorer.

THE ARTS

The Flash

Harry Lampert began drawing cartoon characters Popeye and Betty Boop for New York's Fleischer Studios when he was 16 in 1932. By 1940 he collaborated on the creation of a character that was based on Hermes from Greek mythology that had wings for feet. The Flash was a mild mannered scientist who took on superhero powers as the result of an out of control chemistry experiment. Although The Flash went on to popular acclaim, Harry stopped drawing him after only two issues and became a gag cartoonist for Time, Esquire, The New York Times, the Saturday Evening Post and Saturday Review.

Album Illustrator

Formal painting initially attracted **Thomas B. Allen** to art. He studied at the Art Institute of Chicago in the early 1950's and would break away from painting the romantic notions of life that were featured in magazines such as the Saturday Evening Post to develop a more abstract style. After a string of magazine jobs, Thomas did work for CBS Records that was considered the premier label for graphic design. It was there that he painted the first of many jazz album covers. He was able to meet his subjects and produced colorful portraits of country and western, bluegrass and jazz musicians. He had a passion for the environment that generated his most ambitious visual essay when he retraced, for Esquire magazine, the tracks of painter Frederic Remington through the West in the 19th century.

Influential Ballerina

When she was a child the doctor recommended she take dance lessons to strengthen her frail legs. At the age of 8 she received her first rave review from an annual school performance. In a 52-year career, **Alicia Markova** spanned the ballet companies of Russia, England and the US. She was best associated with the ballet 'Giselle' and was the first British dancer to perform the title role. She became co-founder of the English National Ballet and was a director of the Metropolitan Opera Ballet. A year after her retirement from dancing Alicia was named a Dame of the British Empire.

Unconventional Poet

The nature of poetry was in question. **Jackson Mac Low** was a pioneer who liberated language from logic and into sound and performance. His writing style was unorthodox, he would use words with nonsense syllables and write sentences that ran on for pages. He was considered to be one of the few people who could combine music and word and was a forerunner in conceptual art, sound poetry and performance art. Jackson received the $100,000 Wallace Stevens Award from the Academy of American Poets in 1999.

Made Peter Pan Fly

As a kid he would leap into the air in an attempt to fly and land flat on his face. At 14 he found a more stable opportunity when the stage manager of a school production fell ill and **Peter Foy** took over the responsibility of overseeing the flying actors. His later work with Kirby's Flying Ballet in Britain got him the assignment to come to America and get actress Mary Martin airborne in the 1954 original Broadway musical version of Peter Pan. Peter would establish his own company, Flying by Foy, and work extensively in television and film. He got Sally Field aloft in "The Flying Nun", flew Garth Brooks over Texas Stadium, Nadia Comaneci over Times Square and sent Liberace soaring along with his piano.

Children's Theater

It was dismissed by critics as not worthy of acknowledgment, but **Nellie McCaslin** brought respect to children's theater. As a professor of education theater at New York University, Nellie wrote two college textbooks that are considered classics for the field. She lectured throughout the world and contributed to a better understanding of American educational practices. Nellie firmly believed that theater helps in the emotional, intellectual and social development of a child.

The Tiki Sound

One night during an engagement at a hotel in Hawaii in the mid-1950's, **Martin Denny's** band heard bullfrogs in the background while they played. As a gag, they began to incorporate into their show animal calls and odd musical instruments such as conch shells, Southeast Asian gongs and Japanese kotos and boobams. They took advantage of the new features of stereo recording and created songs and albums that brought the illusion of a restful stop on an exotic island paradise. Their first album, Exotica, went to number 1 on the Billboard charts for five weeks in 1959. Their sound represented the style of Polynesia—tiki cups, Hawaiian shirts and the bikini.

Mad Magazine

It was not his only work, but among his most memorable. For a four-year period between 1958 and 1962, **F. K. Freas** drew the covers of Mad Magazine, including its most illustrious poster boy, Alfred E. Neuman. In all he illustrated more than 300 magazines and won 11 Hugo awards which are considered to be the highest honor for a science fiction artist. Six of his posters for NASA are now in the collection of the Smithsonian Museum. He also drew the portraits of 400 saints for the Franciscans. In 1977, for the rock band Queen, he redrew a 1953 science fiction cover as the album cover for "News of the World" which included their legendary song "We Will Rock You".

Japan's Modern Architect

The country was in ruins after World War II. The city of Hiroshima had essentially been leveled by an atomic bomb in 1945. Four years later **Kenzo Tange** won the competition to build a memorial Peace Park at ground zero in Hiroshima. When the project was completed in 1955 it established Kenzo as the dean of Japanese architects. His status would grow with the twin gymnasiums that curled like commas that were built for the 1964 Olympic Games in Tokyo. He also put his fingerprint on the skylines of Jidda, Saudi Arabia and Singapore. His influence extended to many other Japanese architects in his role as a teacher at Tokyo University. In 1987 he was awarded the Pritzker Prize, architecture's most prestigious award.

Music History Scholar

It was said that his work changed the way people thought and wrote about music. **Stanley Sadie** began as a music critic with the London Times in 1964. When the Macmillan publishing company approached him to edit a new edition of the well regarded Grove Dictionary of Music and Musicians, no one envisioned that he would expand the reference work from 9 volumes to 29 volumes with 97% of it being new material. He also engineered spin-off encyclopedias from the Grove franchise that covered opera, musical instruments and American music. Stanley and his wife's interest in the music of Handel preserved the musician's house in London and led to the creation of the Handel House Museum. Together they also toured 300 composers homes throughout Europe and collaborated on a guidebook, "Calling on the Composer".

The Sparse Poet

The style was called stubbornly plain and made every poem instantly recognizable. To others it was conversational and emotionally direct. **Robert Creeley** was allied with the writers of the Beat Generation and the Black Mountain poets of the 1950's and was an early participant who helped inspire the countercultural revolution of the '60's. Robert received the Bollinger Prize in 1999, poetry's top award. In addition, he was a former chancellor of the Academy of American Poets.

Surrealist Poetry

It was in elementary school that he wrote his first poem. By 15 he became one of the youngest published poets of his generation when **Philip Lamantia** had poems published in a magazine. At 19 he published his first book of poems in 1946. His visionary poems explored the subconscious world of dreams and linked it to the experience of daily life. He had a huge influence on the Beat poets of the 1950's, especially Allen Ginsberg who went on to publish the legendary poem "Howl" after reading Philip's work.

Engraved Postage Stamps

Now it's a faded art, modern printing methods have made its creativity nearly obsolete. But **Czeslaw Slania** produced more than 1,000 customized stamps for 32 countries during his career as a master engraver. His talents required a tool called a 'graver' that cut a mirror image in a steel plate. Deep cuts were used for heavy ink and shallow cuts for shading. The plate, full of ink, was pressed onto the paper as it was printed. For a stamp, the work area for an artist is one inch square. Czeslaw was granted political asylum in Sweden in 1956 from communist Poland. At that point he had worked on 50 Polish stamps. It took several years in Stockholm before he got a full time position as an engraver. Over the next several decades his output became prodigious. Several times Czeslaw was recognized for producing the 'most beautiful stamp of the year'. The king of Sweden appointed him in 1972 as Court Engraver. He became a Knight of the Danish and was also honored by Prince Ranier III of Monaco.

The Origami Master

Origami is the Japanese word for paper folding. It was considered a minor art form associated with children and dated to the Middle Ages. **Akira Yoshizawa** elevated it far beyond the wobbly salt cellars made by kids. He was known for his folding techniques and creating a notation system that made origami instructions universally accessible. Akira's origami was considered structural art, normally made from a single sheet of paper without glue or scissors. He also pioneered a system of notation that permits readers of any language to follow a set of printed instructions. Using dotted lines to indicate the folds and arrows to show the directions of the folds, the system is in wide use today. Another technique was 'wet folding' in which thick paper was dampened slightly and enabled Akira to create a three dimensional form.

Captured Everyday British in Photos

The Independent of London called him "one of the outstanding chroniclers of British life between World War I and II". **Humphrey Spender**'s photographic work reflected the belief that ordinary people are of interest to ordinary people. He roamed the countryside during the Depression years of the 1930's and photographed people, in black and white, as they went about their daily business. Often the camera was concealed under his coat to document the comings and goings of everyday life compiling a chronicle that was rarely featured in the press. His work was seen in the weekly magazine Picture Post and for the pioneering research organization Mass Observation.

Chicano Music

For 60 years **Lalo Guerrero** created songs in Spanish and English that chronicled the Mexican-American experience. He was a self-styled folk musician who made up for his lack of formal training with an ability to capture the essence of Mexican-American life that had been ignored by popular music. Beginning in the 1930's, Lalo was able to compose and sing in an array of styles that earned him the reputation as the Father of Chicano music. He was best known for his 1955 hit, "Pancho Lopez", a parody of the popular song "Davy Crockett". In 1997 he became the first Chicano to receive the National Medal of Arts, presented to him by President Clinton. Nearly 20 years earlier he was named a national folk treasure by the Smithsonian Institution.

Wind Band Conductor

Mozart and Beethoven had written music for wind players, but the works were typically chamber pieces as larger orchestras were known to pit a handful of wind instruments against dozens of violins because the wind section was more powerful. **Frederick Fennell** established himself as the finest wind band conductor since John Philip Sousa when he championed the idea of a wind ensemble with flexible instruments and adaptable layers. The bible of American music, the New Grove Dictionary, said that Frederick created a model for the more than 20,000 wind ensembles that were created in American schools.

Spirit Comic Book

Comics fans called his comic book character the Spirit "The Citizen Kane" of comics for its innovation, seriousness and influence. In June 1940 **Will Eisner** published the first installment of a syndicated comics section that featured a detective who was killed off on the third page. Denny Colt was reborn as a spirit that lacked superpowers and was seen as a middle class crime fighter, a stark departure from the exploits of a comic book character such as Superman. At its height the Spirit appeared in 20 newspapers and reached five million readers every Sunday.

Jazz Organist

The electric organ was considered a novelty in jazz by the 1950's. **Jimmy Smith** made it an important instrument and influenced nearly every subsequent notable organist in jazz and rock. In 1955 Jimmy established an organ trio with a new sound that would become the model for groups in what became known as "organ rooms", the urban bars on the East Coast that specialized in the brand of blues-oriented, swinging, funky music that he created. Many jazz organists were unable to master the bass pedals and used only the keyboards, but Jimmy developed a heel-and-toe technique that played off of his experience as a tap dancer. Jimmy said he always thought of the organ as a horn and strived to create a single line sound like a trumpet.

The Little Drummer Boy

It originated as a Czech carol and was translated into English in 1941 as "Carol of the Drum". It wasn't until 1957 that **Harry Simeone** was approached with the opportunity to record the song. He made a few changes to the arrangement, hired the singers and changed the title to "The Little Drummer Boy". The Harry

Simeone Chorale's version of the song was released the next year on their album "Sing We Now of Christmas" and the song became an instant hit. The Chorale also made popular the Christmas classic "Do You Hear What I Hear".

Besame Mucho

The song is a global phenomenon. It has been translated into dozens of languages and performed by hundreds of artists. It is considered an emblem of Latin identity and an anthem of lovers that were separated during World War II. **Consuelo Velazquez** wrote the song when she was 25 and, as she claimed, had never been kissed. Besame Mucho, or Kiss Me Alot, was recorded in English in 1944 and became a hit for the Jimmy Dorsey Orchestra. The song's haunting melody is based on a Spanish opera from 1916. The song has had more than two million performances on radio and television.

Combined Painting and Architecture

Robert Slutzky was viewed in his profession as a natural person to teach art and the concepts of color and space to architects. His lifelong exploration of the connection between painting and architecture influenced a generation of post World War II architects. It was important for architecture students to understand both how space impacted architecture and also how it was also influenced by painting. Robert was a professor of art and architecture for many years at Cooper Union in New York City. His paintings were concerned with color and form and the relationship between the two. He helped architects bring these issues to their work and trained them to look at, think about and organize space in the same manner as a painter would.

Not Ready for Prime Time Players

His resume included some of television's most famous shows, "The Colgate Comedy Hour", "The Tonight Show" with Steve Allen and later Johnny Carson. "The Perry Como Show" and "That Was the Week That Was" also benefited from his talents. **Herb Sargent** put his lasting mark on television when he was recruited to join a young staff of comedy writers on a new show called "Saturday Night Live". Looking over the cast of unknowns, Herb named them the Not Ready for Prime Time Players. They would develop into some of the medium's legendary performers. He was principally responsible for creating the trademark "Weekend Update" segment that features a lighthearted look at the prior weeks events. Thirty years later it is one of the longest lasting shows in television history. Herb won six Emmy Awards as well as six Writers Guild Awards in his fifty years in the business.

Eskimo Life

Disenchanted with city life, **James Houston** got on a single engine plane in 1948 and flew to an Inuit Eskimo village in the Arctic. He intended to stay for a few days and wound up calling it home for 14 years. He slept in igloos, traveled by dogsled, ate raw seal meat and caribou and climbed 40 foot frozen waterfalls. He became almost single handedly responsible for introducing contemporary Eskimo art to an international audience. He introduced the Eskimos to printmaking, helped them establish a profitable cooperative to sell their prints and sculpture and brought their work to the attention of museums and collectors worldwide. Today, trade in Inuit art runs to over $10 Million annually.

Queen of the Tejano Wave

Tejano music is a combination of Mexican country and traditional folk that has long been popular in borderland ranching areas and small town dance halls. Men tended to dominate the limelight until **Laura Canales** blazed a trail for other female musicians, including the Tejano superstar Selena. Laura made her debut in 1973 and won Female Entertainer and Female Vocalist at the Tejano Music Awards four years in a row in the mid-1980's. She was known as the Barbra Streisand of Tejano music.

The Bassoon

Gwydion Brooke was given a bassoon at age 11 and thought it was a terrible French instrument. He struggled through and earned a scholarship to the Royal Academy of Music in England. In 1932 he joined the London Philharmonic and a few years later the BBC Scottish Radio Orchestra. He was considered one of the most influential instrumentalists of the 20th century. Gwydion developed such techniques as a rapid double tonguing and a sensuous vibrato. He formed a group called the Rhythm Classics and, using these techniques, the group became very popular and was on the radio on a regular basis. Gwydion radically altered his instrument through the years and added keys and finger holes that were re-bored in new positions. They created his signature sound, but his bassoon was unplayable to anyone else.

British Pop Art

He was considered one of the most inventive, prolific sculptors of the post-World War II era in Great Britain. **Eduardo Paolozzi** was also a highly original print-maker, some of his collage-based silkscreen images are among the finest examples of British pop art, a style that he was integral in shaping. It was in Paris that Eduardo produced rudimentary collages from advertisements in American glossy magazines. They were made mainly for his own amusement, but today they are regarded as important early examples of pop art. In sculpture, he became renowned for taking objects out of their context and placing them in new combinations, giving them new meaning. He would take pieces of machinery and cast them in aluminum. He would then join them together by welding, drilling and bolting. The result was described as totems for the technology age.

Helped Develop Public TV

WQED in Pittsburgh was the first community owned television station in the United States and a promising source of original programming for educational TV. In 1955, **John White** arrived to become the general manager. During this same time period, the National Educational TV and Radio Center had been formed originally as a clearinghouse for university-owned TV stations to exchange programs. They would produce five hours of its own programs and mail them to other stations. John moved to head up the Center in 1958. He dropped the radio programming, solicited corporate donations and turned the operation into NET, National Educational Television, as a forerunner of PBS. When he left in 1969, NET had 161 affiliated stations to which it fed cultural and public affairs TV programming.

Dean of Magic

It was a lifelong attraction. At age 7 he saw Houdini perform, but fell asleep. He traded away his bicycle to buy a mail order magic course. **Jay Marshall** was elected dean of the Society of Magicians in 1992, only the 8th in the history of the organization. A writer, collector and editor of anything having to do with magic, he owned one of the US' largest magic stores. He was valued for his immense knowledge going back to the glory years of vaudeville. Jay was among the best known and most booked magicians of his day. He appeared on the Ed Sullivan show 14 times as well as playing the Palace in New York and the Palladium in London.

Walt Disney Storyteller

He was one of the most extraordinary artists and story men to ever work at the Walt Disney Studios. His career there spanned almost seven decades. For Snow White and the Seven Dwarfs, **Joe Grant** designed the queen and her alter ego, the wicked witch, who was based on a neighbor across the street from his home. In quick succession he guided the creation of Fantasia, Pinocchio and Dumbo. Several years later in 1955, Joe and his wife conceived Lady and The Tramp. With his vast knowledge of art and literature, he was considered the Studio's top intellectual and he had a profound influence on films that he made. In later years Joe was involved with Beauty and the Beast, Aladdin and The Lion King. In 1992 he was named a Disney legend. More than 70 of his caricatures are permanently exhibited at the Smithsonian.

Bluegrass Singer

His first guitar consisted of rubber bands stretched across a flat tin Prince Albert tobacco can. He hunted and sold possum skins to buy a guitar at age 10. By age 21 **Jimmy Martin** was fired from singing on the job at a factory. His next step was to visit the Grand Ole Opry in Nashville and audition for his idol, Bill Monroe. Jimmy performed as a vocalist for Bill's band from 1949 to 1954 before forming his own band, the Sunny Mountain Boys. Although he was never extremely popular in the commercial country music industry, his peers rated Jimmy as among the foremost bluegrass musicians of the 20th century. His musical ability and hillbilly personality endeared him to audiences. In 1995 he was inducted into the International Bluegrass Music Association's Hall of Honor.

Sports Action Photographer

The New York Daily Mirror was the first stop as a sportswriter during the Depression. When he saw that he could make more money in photography, **Hy Peskin** switched for a salary of $21 a week. He was a loner and sought out unusual vantage points at a time when sports photographers normally stayed together in the press box. Hy was the first to move down to the field and shoot at ground level. In 1954 he became the first staff photographer hired by Sports Illustrated. He would shoot 40 covers for them and freelance for other national magazines such as Time. Life and Look. Hy was credited with taking the first action photo in color, a boxing match in 1945. Sports Illustrated cited two of his pictures on its list of favorite sports photos of the 20th century.

Movie Makeup Artist

While still a teenager, **Bob Schiffer** worked as a seaman on an ocean liner and earned money by making up passengers for costume balls. He started his professional career at 18 when his job was to apply makeup to hundreds of extras that were being thrown to the lions in the movie "The Last Days of Pompeii". He moved on to RKO Studios and worked on Hollywood's first picture made in color, "Becky Sharp" in 1935. The years ahead would find Bob working on countless classic films including the Fred Astaire-Ginger Rogers series, The Hunchback of Notre Dame, The Wizard of Oz and My Fair Lady among many others. He became Rita Haworth's exclusive makeup artist for 20 years and formed a long association with Burt Lancaster. By 1968 Bob moved to Walt Disney Studios where he became head of the makeup department and spent the last 33 years of his career there. In 2001 he received the Lifetime Achievement Award from the Hollywood Makeup Artist and Hair Stylist Guild.

Furniture Designer

She was remarkable for being a woman in the male dominated world of industrial design. Working in materials ranging from fiber glass to foam rubber to make tables, chairs and sofas for homes and offices, **Nanna Ditzel** was a leading member of the generation of designers who created the postwar modern movement in Denmark and was called the "First Lady of Danish Furniture Design". Her work spanned a number of areas in innovative accessories including interiors, ceramics, textiles and jewelry. Nanna's work was displayed in art centers around the word including New York, London, Madrid and Milan.

For The Troops

"I'm in the Mood for Love" was singer/actress **Frances Langford**'s greatest hit song. She first performed it in 1935 for the movie "Every Night at Eight". She gained her greatest admiration for her courage in touring abroad during three periods of wartime. With Bob Hope, during World War II she entertained the troops at bases in England, Africa, Sicily, the Caribbean and the Pacific and was given the nickname, "sweetheart of the fighting fronts". When she returned to New York City she wrote a 'Purple Heart Diary' for the Journal-American newspaper about her experiences visiting servicemen who had been wounded. In 1952 Frances and a troupe of entertainers spent six weeks in Korea performing for GI's. They visited every division and unit along the 155-mile front. In 1966 she was part of a group who entertained troops in Vietnam for several weeks.

Superman

Paul Cassidy was a graphics arts teacher at a Milwaukee vocational school when he was offered the opportunity to join a Superman comic book artist's studio in Cleveland in 1938. Paul was assigned to do the ink and detail work and added a more fluid line to the comic book character's appearance with a bolder, darker style. He added the famous 'S' to Superman's cape and made it more dynamic by adding folds and wrinkles to it. His time with the studio was short, lasting only two years due to a low salary, but Paul's contributions stood the test of time.

Screenwriter

Liberty magazine bought his first creative writing story in 1943. For the next ten years **Ernest Lehman** worked as a freelancer writing stories, novellas and radio comedy. Paramount brought him to Hollywood in 1953 after a short story of his appeared in Collier's magazine. He started out with a six-month contract, but would go on to receive four Academy Award nominations for best screenplay and two nominations as a producer. Ernest adapted for the screen such classics as "West Side Story", "Virginia Woolf", "The Sound of Music", "The King and I" and "Sweet Smell of Success". His best-known credit was his original screenplay for "North by Northwest". In his career Ernest received five Writers Guild of America awards along with nine nominations. The Guild gave him their prestigious Screen Laurel Award in 1972. In 2001 Ernest became the first screenwriter to receive a lifetime achievement award from the Academy of Motion Picture Arts and Sciences.

Mentor to Rock Legends

The rhythm and blues artist "Leadbelly" was his first influence. At 14 **John Baldry** bought a guitar and learned to play a 12 string in his style. By 1962 he had become the lead singer with a band in London called the Alexis Korner Blues Incorporated. Members of that band included Mick Jagger and Charlie Watts who would shortly lead their own band, The Rolling Stones. A few years later John had joined another group and one day heard a 19-year-old singing on a train platform in London. John brought him into the group as a secondary singer, his name was Rod Stewart. Later on a new band John was with had a young keyboardist who decided to use John's first name as one of two name's the keyboardist would use for his soon to be established solo act. He would later on be known as Elton John.

Rock 'n' Roll Writer

His early work was groundbreaking for its ability to connect developments in music and society. It began in the early 1960's with articles for The Saturday Evening Post that studied the pop music business and the personalities behind it. By 1963 **Al Aronowitz** was writing about the kingpins of teen pop such as Carole King and Don Kirschner and was recognized as one of the first professional journalists to cover rock 'n' roll. The following year he covered the arrival of the Beatles in the United States and introduced Bob Dylan to the group while they were staying in New York City. By the late '60's writing about rock music in a serious, critical manner was just emerging and Al was considered a pioneer at the craft.

Developed a System for Composing

Lyle "Spud" Murphy was a prolific composer who created more than 250 stock arrangements for several leading music publishers. Many are still in use today by dance bands around the world. For big band leader Benny Goodman alone he composed more than 100 arrangements in the 1930's and 40's. Spud's system of composing became widely used by musicians. His method was a simple way to deal with 12 notes by using six intervals. By mastering the six intervals, a composer would be able to write any style or type of music freely. Spud was persuaded to teach his method under the G.I. bill and would train hundreds of students in his method. Among his many commercial works was turning the children's song "Three Blind Mice" into the theme for the Three Stooges shows.

Bossa Nova

Keter Betts played with the greats of jazz. He was an upright bass player who spent more than two decades accompanying and touring with Ella Fitzgerald. Other jazz artists he worked with included Stan Gertz, Charlie Byrd, Nat Adderley, Dinah Washington and Oscar Peterson. It was on an extended trip to South America in 1961 that he heard the Brazilian rhythms of bossa nova. On his return to the United States he joined forces with two other musicians in releasing the album, "Jazz Samba" that helped to start the worldwide bossa nova phenomenon.

Photographed Older Women

Anne Noggle described her subjects as the "saga of the fallen flesh". She focused her photography on the effects of aging and the imperfections they created. Anne believed that when women reached a certain age they became unseen and unheard. In the early 1970's she used her own mother as one of her main subjects and took photos of herself to mark the passage of years. Over a two-decade period she received several grants including three from the National Endowment for the Arts and a Guggenheim Fellowship. Anne also taught at the University of New Mexico for 14 years.

Disneyland

The only tool he used was a slide rule in the era before computer animation. Walt Disney handpicked **Fred Joerger** in 1953 to become one of his first three model makers. The three invented a profession that would be known as Imagineering, a Disney term for the imagination and engineering that go into developing theme park rides. Fred's work provided the foundations for Disneyland. The first model he made was the steamboat Mark Twain and was followed by Main Street, the Jungle Cruise, the Matterhorn and much of the rest of the original amusement park. He came out of retirement in the early 1980's to oversee the look of Disney's Epcot Center in Florida.

Polish Posters

Before World War II Polish advertising posters were as attention grabbing in appearance as any in Europe. Following the devastation of the war, more somber posters appeared that reflected the country's domination by the Soviet Union. At the time, posters served as an important way to communicate information to the public. Brushes and paint was scarce and printing and paper were not up to standards. With these dreary conditions, **Henryk Tomaszewski** created bold colors and abstract shapes to achieve graphic power. His animated and witty posters for the movies, circus and theater led to the distinctive Polish Poster School style and his work would become recognized throughout the world.

African-American Children's Books

Picture books featuring or including minority children were largely absent before the 1960's. The industry was criticized for being prejudiced and a few books featuring minorities began to appear at that time. **Toni Trent Parker** helped to significantly advance the cause of books focusing on African-American children when she and two friends established a company to promote her books. In 1998 she introduced a series of four guides to black children's books. That same year she established the non-profit Kids Cultural Books to hold book festivals around the US to bring multicultural books and their authors together. In 2000 the organization was given a grant from the prestigious John and Catherine MacArthur Foundation.

Organ Builder

By demonstrating a grasp of the classic principles of an organ, **Noel Mander** was in the forefront of their design and restoration. He earned a reputation as a restorer with sensitivity. While in North Africa during World War II, he restored an organ in Algiers Cathedral that had been silent for decades. Returning to London after the war, Noel's recognition grew as he repaired many of the city's bomb damaged church organs. One of his projects required work on a 17th century instrument once played by Handel. His greatest effort came with the five-year creation of a new chamber organ for St. Paul's Cathedral that was completed in 1981 and first played at the wedding of Prince Charles and Princess Diana.

BUSINESS

California Winemaker

Timothy Diener was a member of the De La Salle Christian Brothers for 75 years. His first assignment was to teach high school chemistry in the San Francisco Bay area. In 1935, two years after the end of Prohibition, he became a wine chemist at the brother's vineyards in Napa Valley. Profits from winemaking went to schools on the West Coast and paid for a retreat house and summer camps. He helped to reestablish the image of California winemaking while emerging from Prohibition. Sales were initially at 10,000 gallons per year, but grew significantly in later years. In 1987 the California Vintners Association honored him as a Living Legend.

Universal Studio Tour

An outdated commissary sitting on the lot of Universal Studios was presenting a problem for **Albert Dorskind**. It was losing $100,000 a year in the early 1960's for his company, MCA. One weekend he was walking through the Farmers Market in Los Angeles and saw a group of tourists having lunch. Albert came up with the idea to have tourists eat lunch at the Universal commissary while watching the activity on the back lot of a major Hollywood studio. He contacted the Gray Line bus company and the first tours began. The chairman of MCA was convinced to make backlot improvements to accommodate the tourists and trams were designed to transport them around the lot. The modern Universal Studios tour was begun on July 4, 1964. Today it is one of California's top tourist attractions.

The First Video Rental Store

To people under a certain age it's hard to imagine a time without movie videos and DVD's. The first VCR was introduced in 1975 and two years later **George Atkinson** thought he would test a theory. Without any videos, he placed a 'Video for Rent' ad in the newspaper asking people to mail a coupon back to him. Within a week he had a thousand coupons. He then bought 50 movies that had recently become available and began renting movies for $10 a day. With rapid sales, George opened the first of what would become 600 Video Station rental stores. He was inducted into the Video Hall of Fame in 1991. Today there are 24,000 video stores in the United States that rent 2.6 billion DVDs and cassettes each year.

Bundt Cake Pan

In the late 1940's **H. David Dalquist** and his wife began manufacturing bake ware. A few years later they were approached by a women's volunteer society who were looking to have a pan made that could fit the dense cakes they were making based on their German grandmother's recipes. He produced a pan made in cast aluminum and also began to sell the pan in department stores, calling it a "bundt pan" from the German word 'bund' meaning bond or alliance. The pans didn't sell very well until 1966 when a Texas woman used a bundt pan to win second place in the Pillsbury Bake-Off contest. Pillsbury was inundated with 200,000 inquiries asking where the pan could be purchased. David's company began producing 30,000 pans a day. It is estimated that his company eventually sold more than 45 million.

Mae West Vest

He worried his mother at age 16 when he bought a boat and substantially increased its power. To stop her from thinking he might drown, **Andrew Toti** designed a flotation device that was filled with duck feathers. He would later change it to air because the original was too bulky. The War Department found out about his invention and paid him $1,600 for the rights to mass-produce them. It was called the 'Mae West vest' because of the bulk it created in the chest area that reminded people of the movie star. Among the beneficiaries of the vest was President George H. W. Bush who was wearing one when he was shot down over the Pacific during World War II. Descendants of the vest are still in use today. Through his career, Andrew accumulated more than 500 patents, including an automated feather plucker that used thousands of rubber fingers that were quicker than the human hand. The invention revolutionized the poultry business. In 2004, the Andrew Toti Museum of Innovations opened near Modesto, California.

Popularized Binoculars

Before **David Bushnell**'s honeymoon through Shanghai in 1947, binoculars were toys for the rich. An importer/exporter, David shipped 400 pairs to the United States and marketed them to spectators at the Santa Anita horse racetrack in Southern California. He authorized an advertisement that read: "The world is beautiful. See it up close". Sales were so brisk that he abandoned selling any other products except the binoculars. Post World War II labor was cheap in Japan and Hong Kong and David passed on the savings to the American consumer. The original company was sold in 1971 and it is estimated that the current version of the company sells more than half of all binoculars bought in the United States.

Year Round Flowers

While British expatriates were leaving Kenya in the mid 1960's, **John Addington** stayed on and bought a nursery. He soon ran the nursery and grew carnations, roses and other flowers. John organized the difficult task of importing and repacking them in Britain. The venture was an immediate success and the Dutch, who were leaders in the international flower export business, soon followed his example. Eventually John left Kenya to run a 26-acre site in England. His business played an important role in making cut flowers a familiar feature through all seasons the year-round. On the death of his father in 1967, John became Lord Sidmouth and took his seat in the House of Lords.

Municipal Bonds

In the 1970's municipal bond issues often amounted to $100 Million and insuring them was too expensive for any one company. **William Bailey** was an executive with the Aetna Life and Casualty Company who convinced four other firms to jointly offer state and local governments insurance that would guarantee the repayment of money loaned to them by investors. The newly created Municipal Bond Insurance Association was started in 1973 and allowed municipalities to borrow money from the public at lower interest rates. It helped to create an industry that has insured more than $2 Trillion and has saved taxpayers $35 Billion in interest that would have been paid on uninsured bonds.

Stock Car Racing

He started out building race cars with a partner in the 1940's. Nearly ten years later they bought race tracks in Richmond, VA and Wilson, NC. **Paul Sawyer** bought out his partner the following year and eventually turned a regional sport into an international phenomenon. The Wilson location closed and he concentrated his efforts on the Richmond speedway. In 1968 he paved over the dirt track with a half-mile of asphalt. Twenty years later he turned the track into a D-shaped three-quarter mile track and expanded seating to 47,500. By the time he sold his interest in the raceway in 1999 the Richmond International Speedway had a capacity of 110,000 and was considered one of the country's finest auto racing venues. Paul received a NASCAR Founders Award and the Buddy Shuman Award which is presented for having made a significant contribution to the growth of NASCAR.

Architect of a Landmark

He designed 280 buildings in the southeast Los Angeles area. **Paul Clayton**'s most recognized work was "Johnnie's Broiler", a hugely popular center of the Southern California car culture in the 1950's and 1960's. Johnnie's was a uniquely designed coffee shop that has qualified for the California Register of Historic Resources. During the 1960's it would draw up to 5,000 customers a weekend to its location in Downey where teenagers gathered to check out their cars and one another over hamburgers and sodas. Johnnie's was typical of what is known as the Southern California 'Googie' design in which the entire building is basically a sign to attract customers. They often include dramatic rooflines, glass walls, V-shaped car canopies and open cooking stations that combine to give off a Space Age appearance.

Miracle-Gro

In the mid-1940's a nurseryman in New York asked ad agency salesman **Horace Hagedorn** to help him sell his mail order plants and trees which were not doing too well. They decided fertilizer might work and approached a college professor to help develop a water-soluble fertilizer. Horace' wife came up with the name Miracle-Gro and the company was formed in 1950. Horace served as the creative force and became the marketing whiz of the operation. Miracle-Gro became a familiar site in the American backyard. Today the gardening business is estimated at $35 Billion and Miracle-Gro's share of the home fertilizer market is 85 percent.

Intermittent Windshield Wipers

The thought came to him at the strangest time. On his wedding day in 1953 a champagne cork hit **Robert Kearns** in the eye. While he was consciously blinking he wondered if windshield wipers would work the same way by moving at intervals and not the typical back and forth motion. He experimented with the concept for years and then approached Ford in the early 1960's. The engineers sent him out of the room because they were convinced he was activating the wipers with a button in his pocket. Ford took what appeared to be a pass on Robert's invention. By 1967 Robert received the first of more than 30 patents for his wipers. Two years later Ford came out with their own version of the intermittent wipers and was followed by other carmakers a few years later, but no one credited Robert for his work. Lawsuits followed over the next two decades with Robert eventually receiving settlements from Ford and Chrysler.

Sleek Designs

It took just two weeks to create one of the world's most consummate sports cars, the Studebaker Avanti. **John Ebstein** led a team of Chrysler designers that had to come up with an answer to the Ford Thunderbird. It had a Coke-bottle shape with a narrowing in the middle that inspired European racing cars for a generation. It could hold four passengers and had two doors, a long hood, a host trunk, an asymmetrical power bulge on the hood, virtually no chrome and no fins. The interior was inspired by aircraft flight decks with numerous toggle switches on the console. It became revered among automobile enthusiasts and design devotees. In his career as an industrial designer John also influenced the appearance of Air Force One, space capsules, Greyhound buses and Lucky Strike cigarettes.

Interior Designer

She was known for creating elegant spaces for prominent retailers. **Naomi Leff** created a following when, in 1986, she transformed a mansion in New York City into the flagship store for Polo Ralph Lauren. Her earlier work had included designing interiors for Neiman-Marcus, Bergdorf Goodman and Bloomingdale's. She was known to capture almost any era or mood and used every style from neo-classic beachfront estates and Art Deco apartments to English country cottages and dude ranches. Naomi was repeatedly listed among the top names in her field by Architectural Digest and Interior Design magazines.

Little Oscar

In 1936 the nephew of Oscar Mayer came up with the idea of a Wienermobile, a 22-foot long, 10-foot high hot dog on wheels. During the same year a man who would later play one of the munchkins in the Wizard of Oz met with **George**

Molchan in his small Indiana hometown to convince him that his shortness should not deter him in life. Fifteen years later George was contacted by the same man who urged him to become a Little Oscar. For twenty years he crisscrossed the United States in the Wienermobile handing out hot-dog shaped Magic Wiener Whistles. During the week he would visit small stores, schools, orphanages and children's hospitals and spent the weekend at major grocery chains and parades and festivals. After leaving the Wienermobile George spent another 16 years greeting patrons at the company's restaurant at Disney World.

Organic Farm

Paul Keene was educated as a mathematician and became a missionary and teacher in India in the late 1930's where he met Ghandi who advised him to give everything away. Paul also discovered the work of the founder of the worldwide organic farming movement. Returning to the US, Paul and his wife bought a 108 acre farm in the mid-1940's and worked the land without tractors or electricity and grew crops without the artificial fertilizers and pesticides that were widely used by other farmers. The apples they grew at their Walnut Acres farm were the first food in the country to be certified as organic. By 2000, Walnut Acres Farm was mailing about one million catalogues a year and offering more than 700 products. Today there are about 900 organic farms in the US with annual sales of $12 billion.

Matchbox Cars

For several decades after World War II **Leslie Smith** was the world's largest carmaker because he made the world's smallest autos. His company introduced the miniature car in 1953 with a version of Queen Elizabeth II's coronation coach. More than one million sold. The best-known cars normally measured about three inches long and were designed to fit into a British matchbox. The first set of cars included a dump truck, cement mixer and road roller. In 1956 they introduced the Models of Yesteryear based on turn-of-the-century autos. By 1962, the company was producing 50 million cars a year, more than all of the world's major automakers combined. To make the cars, the designers visited carmakers, vintage car museums and private collectors. They would take many photographs and even obtain blueprints. The result was a scale model that was normally one-sixty-fourth the size of the real car, a palm sized model with wheels that turned and, in later years, doors, hoods and trunks that opened. Leslie was granted the Order of the British Empire in 1968.

Coin Collector

Already a stamp collector as a teenager, in his first coin transaction **John Ford, Jr.** paid fifteen cents for a Confederate bill that years later would earn him $200. Among the collection he would assemble were notes of Massachusetts issued in 1690, the oldest coins issued by the Continental Congress and an African chief's medals. John's impact on the field of coin collecting stemmed from his catalogs. His meticulous descriptions of grades, colors and other qualities represented some of the highest coin scholarship in the United States. John also contributed to in-depth coin collecting research at the National Archives.

TV Dinners

At the time of his creation in the early 1950's he didn't even own a TV set. Swanson & Sons had a dilemma. They had 500,000 pounds of unsold Thanksgiving turkeys that were being sent back and forth across the country in refrigerated railroad cars. **Gerry Thomas** was a salesman for the company and had recently gotten a sample aluminum meal tray that Pan Am airlines was planning to use to serve hot food on overseas flights. He converted the tray into three compartments and convinced the company to fill it with their excess turkey. In 1954 the first Swanson TV dinner was sold for 98 cents in a box designed to look like a television screen. It consisted of turkey, cornbread dressing and gravy, buttered peas and sweet potatoes. 10 million cartons disappeared from grocery store shelves in the first 10 months. Today frozen foods bring in $30 billion a year. Gerry became a member of the Frozen Food Hall of Fame, was awarded a star on the Hollywood Walk of Fame, with his handprints next to a tray, and was recognized by the men's magazine Maxim as one of the "50 Greatest Guys of the Century".

Charlie the Tuna

The Leo Burnett advertising agency was well known for its creation of such legendary ad characters as Tony the Tiger, the Marlboro Man and the Jolly Green Giant. **Tom Rogers** joined the agency in Chicago in the early 1960's and was responsible for the creative piece of the Starkist Tuna account. The result was Charlie the Tuna, based on an acquaintance of his who frequented the beat scene in 1950's New York City. Tom had total control over the Charlie character: how he looked, the sound of his voice and what he said about the product. Charlie appeared in 86 commercials and guest spots during the 60's and 70's before he was retired as the Starkist spokesman. Although he did not create the characters,

Tom also had a hand in developing ad mascots the Keebler elves and Morris the Cat.

Pioneer CPA

Life began in the segregated South of Mississippi. Following high school graduation, **Mary Washington** went to work at one of the country's largest African-American owned banks. Influenced by a supervisor, she earned a college degree at Northwestern University in Illinois and began an accounting practice at night in her basement. A 1943 study by the National Association of Black Accountants determined that Mary was the first African-American woman Certified Public Accountant in the United States. By 1968, with a group of partners she founded an accounting firm in Chicago. Mary had retired by 1985 and the practice still remains today as one of the nation's largest African-American owned accounting companies.

Publishing Empire

In the early 1940's a civil rights leader told him that a black oriented magazine would never sell. Using his mother's furniture as security for a $500 loan, **John Johnson** began publishing a magazine for African-Americans in 1942. Working at a black-owned life insurance company, he asked 20,000 policyholders for a $2 subscription fee. 3,000 responded and he published Negro Digest, modeled on Readers Digest. With that success John created a second magazine based on the popular Life and Look magazines of the time. Ebony debuted and sold out its initial run of 25,000 copies. In the early 1950's Jet magazine was added. It was said that Rosa Parks was inspired not to give up her seat on a Birmingham bus because of Jet's coverage of the lack of civil rights for black people. Other publications and business ventures came in the years ahead that made John in 1982 the first African-American to make the Forbes list of the 400 wealthiest Americans. By 1986 he was awarded the Presidential Medal of Freedom by President Clinton.

Spoonplugs

As a longtime fisherman, **Elwood Perry** concluded that fish move predictably along routes that are influenced by underwater conditions and follow the contours in a lake or stream. He determined that they spent most of their time in deep water and become active when they move up to more shallow water. To figure out where a fresh water fish would be, Elwood developed a combination of a spoon and a plug that he patented in 1946 as the "Spoonplug". He called it "a shoehorn that's been tromped on by a horse". It was designed to find fish and get them to nibble. There were seven sizes, the largest for deep water. Elwood was called the father of structured fishing for the system he created to get fish to bite. Sales took off in 1957 after he demonstrated his technique to a couple of Chicago writers in a lake that supposedly had no fish. Spoonplugs are still commercially available today.

Changed the Nature of Home Building

In the past the roof of a new home was built with individual rafters in a process that required highly skilled carpenters who could make precise cuts and had to drive the nails into the lumber at a sharp angle which made it very time consuming. Sitting in church one day in 1950, **J. Calvin Jureit** came up with the idea for the Gang-Nail Connector Plate, a simple to use device to connect roof trusses. The plate was compared to Henry Ford's assembly line in its impact on making home production more efficient. There were other similar devices on the market by the mid-50's, but his connector required no nailing, gluing, or drilling. With the roof truss industry booming at the time, it had a major impact on home building.

Reflective Signs

Working for the 3M company in 1937, **Harry Heltzer** was assigned a project to make the center stripe on the highway shine brighter than the standard white or yellow paint on the road. He made his own small glass beads and created a double-coated tape with the beads on one side and an adhesive on the other. The tape wouldn't stick on the cold Minnesota roads where he lived so Harry came up with a striping that would stick to the road's surface. He eventually was awarded six patents for reflective highway products that aided drivers in navigating the road at night.

EDUCATION

Forensic Psychiatrist

Considered a pioneer by introducing psychology into legal policy, **Lawrence Freedman** investigated the causes of violence. He focused on the dark world of assassinations, terrorism and mass murder. In the 1950's and 60's Lawrence created a legal standard for insanity while a member of the Model Penal Code's Criminal Law Advisory Committee. Many states adopted parts of the code which was intended to be a model statute to standardize criminal penalties. He believed that the role of the mental health professional should be to tell the jury, without bias, the working of a person's mind at the time of the crime. Lawrence was appointed by President Lyndon Johnson to the National Commission on Causes and Prevention of Violence and developed a psychological profile of potential assassins for the Secret Service following the death of President John Kennedy.

Cartographer

For over 2,500 years map makers have struggled with the format to depict the Earth as a sphere on a flat piece of paper. In the 1500's the Flemish cartographer Mercator created a map that made Greenland four times its actual size and appeared larger than South America. It became the standard map for centuries. **Arthur Robinson** developed an ability for mapmaking while he earned a masters degree at the University of Wisconsin. In 1963 he created a map he called 'the world as it really is". The National Geographic Society endorsed his map 25 years later as a 'more realistic' version of what the magazine had offered in the past. Arthur's map was also selected by the Pentagon for its briefing room.

Psychoanalyst

He was confused as a young boy when he would watch his mother cry at the end of a movie. Over five decades **Joseph Weiss** developed the 'control master theory' which said that patients enter therapy with the unconscious intention of exploring and replaying past traumas. The therapist is used by the patient to test and disprove ideas that may have been blocking the development of the patient's behavior. Joseph promoted the view that if the therapist responded to the patient in a manner that was counter to their negative perceptions of the event they would be able to grow psychologically.

Social Scientist

Otis Duncan was an early advocate of quantitative sociology which involves looking for numerical comparisons to analyze social trends. In a 1967 investigation of social standing, Otis found that a parent's monetary status had an influence on a child's future social standing, but education was a stronger influence. He was the first person to determine that freedom and opportunity are not always tied to social origins.

New Geometry

Shiing-Sen Chern was a mathematician whose discoveries about the shapes of surfaces found wide applications in physics and math. He worked in a field called differential geometry in which the curve of a surface can give an indication of its overall shape. His work led to improvements in the fields of string theory, theoretical physics and computer graphics. He helped to create three mathematics institutes, two in China and one in the United States. Shiing-Sen received the Medal of Science in 1975 and the Wolf Prize which is considered to be one of the highest honors in math.

Expanded the Minds of Children

100 books over 50 years. All written for children to help them learn about animals and concepts like space and time. **Miriam Schlein** would educate and entertain with her stories and clear up myths about animals. She wrote about a diverse array of creatures: elephants, pandas, sea horses, pigeons and squirrels. Several of her natural science books received Outstanding Science Book for Children awards.

Chaos Theory for Babies

The conventional thinking was that infants reached out and walked when the parts of their brain responsible for those functions became mature. As a developmental psychologist, **Esther Thelen** felt that her 'applied dynamic systems theory' understood the overall behavior of the child's system by investigating how the parts of the whole come together. This interplay would give an indication of how they would adapt later in life. Her 'chaos theory' changed therapists' approach as they began to design individual exercises for the child's body and not use a standard exercise for all children of a certain age.

The Linguist

Developing a stammer in elementary school, **George Campbell** was ignored by his teachers and sent to the back of the classroom. He used the time productively by reading. When he rode his bike to school he propped a language book up on his handlebars to read. He would go on to speak and write fluently in 44 languages with a working knowledge of an additional 20. He authored "The Compendium of the World's Languages" that included articles on more than 250 tongues. George was identified by the Guinness Book of World Records in the 1980's as one of the world's greatest living linguists.

Economist

Gerard Debreu believed that mathematicians did not do a good job of explaining to the public how math connects with everyday life. The winner of the 1983 Nobel Prize in Economics, his math models showed how prices function to balance what producers supply with what buyers want. Computer models based on his work are routinely used by the World Bank and other government agencies to analyze trends in national economies and world markets.

The Stone Age

His interest in the Paleolithic Age first began while he was writing a book on the US space program. **Alexander Marshack** went to southwest France in the 1960's to analyze the small incisions in the plaque of bones that dated back 30,000 years to the last part of the ice age during the Paleothic Period. Most anthropologists and archaeologists thought that they were only decorative markings. Alexander determined that they were lunar calendars and established that human beings were keeping records 25,000 years before the start of formal writing and 20,000 years before the start of agriculture. This changed the perception of Stone Age man to the realization that they were more inventive than previously thought.

Educational Filmmaker

During World War II **Sy Wexler** was a cameraman for the Academy Award winning director Frank Capra during the making of his well-known documentary 'Why We Fight'. Although that was the closest Sy would ever get to Hollywood, his 300 educational, training and documentary films over a 35 year-period were still able to reach millions and bring a message. It was a time before the Internet and CD-ROM's and schools and business needed to get information out to large numbers of people. Such varied titles as "High Blood Pressure", "How a Hamburger Turns into You" and "Squeak the Squirrel", delivered in 16 millimeter black-and-white films that ran anywhere from 10 to 30 minutes, brought value to numerous topics that served the education and medical communities.

Childhood Development

Sheldon White believed that research should have a practical use and spent his career turning study findings into educational policy and practice. As a developmental psychologist at Harvard University in the 1960's, Sheldon gained prominence for his studies on how children learn. The findings contributed to the creation of the Head Start program. He worked with children aged 5 to 7 and studied their eye movements and the effects of other stimuli that attracted their attention. He worked with the Children's Television Workshop at the time that CTW was developing Sesame Street. Sheldon also investigated how children learn ethical standards.

Cognitive Psychology

Cognition is the process that weaves strands of memory, perception and judgment into coherent thought. In the mid-1950's, **Howard Gruber** made a trip to Europe to study the unpublished notebooks of Charles Darwin. This led to an in-depth analysis of how Darwin's ideas developed. Almost twenty years later, Howard's book on the study of Darwin's creativity, "Darwin on Man", was named by American Scientist as one of the most important scientific books of the 20th century. Among the book's achievements was the demonstration of the slow, integrative processes of creative thought which come about by solving many problems and not just having one "breakthrough" moment of thought.

Graph Theory

Graph theory dates from the 18th century and focuses on the edges and vertices that are found in graphs. It is frequently used to model physical or abstract problems in such diverse areas as chemistry, computer networks, transportation lines and sociology. It explains mathematically the relationship among individuals. Solutions to problems can appear as theorems or algorithms. **Frank Harary**'s 1969 book on graph theory was credited with giving the field a broader relevance. He lectured in more than 80 countries on the subject and wrote 700 academic papers. Frank also co-authored books about structural models in mathematics and the field of graphical enumeration.

Gardens and Healthy Eating for Kids

They called her "the teacher who loves bugs". **Christina Korten** founded the Nutrition Network to educate children about healthy eating and used school gardens planted with fruits and vegetables as a primary teaching tool. To help the Los Angeles schools fund a gardening program, Christina became a founding member of an education partnership that attracted 50 agricultural agencies to contribute materials and offer workshops on various garden-related topics. The Nutrition Network was formed as an innovative way to help increase the number of school gardens in LA public schools. Its goal is to teach children the value of a diet rich in fruits and vegetables and to promote the benefits of physical exercise. The Network was established by federal grants and today 300 of the 500 school districts in LA who qualify now participate.

The Little Red School House

Ruth Pease was providing daycare at her home in Los Angeles in the early 1940's. With the US at war, she looked after a child whose father was Chinese and mother was white. They had been unable to find daycare and Ruth thought people believed he was Japanese. Ruth's attitude was that every child had a right to be cared for. Eventually Ruth was caring for six children and started a nursery in their house that her husband painted red. They called their business the "Small Fry Nursery School", but it soon became identified as "the little red schoolhouse". A storybook bell tower was added to the house and the name was officially changed. The school grew to 20 children in the 1950's and the children reflected a diverse range of the socioeconomic status of the area. In 1951 Ruth helped form the Pre-School Association of California to lobby for higher standards and closer monitoring of preschools and nursery schools. Ruth and her husband retired in the 1980's. Today the school has five buildings and 250 students in classes from preschool to the eighth grade and is now known as the Hollywood Schoolhouse.

Category Theory

The language of modern math depends upon **Saunders Mac Lane**'s work. Category theory was first developed as a language to describe transformations from one area of math to another. He became one of the pioneers of a subject that changes structures that are seen as shapes and converts them into algebra structures. The theory has been used in fields as diverse as linguistics, mathematical physics and computer science. Saunders received the highest award for scientific achievement in 1989, the National Medal of Sciences.

Economist Analyzed Poverty and Wealth

He advocated dependency theory which said that rich, developed countries gained from poor and underdeveloped countries as long as those countries stayed within the global system of capitalism. **Andre Gunder Frank** was considered to be ahead of his time. Many of his predictions about the developing world have proven to be accurate such as the continuation of poverty despite foreign investment, the failure of capitalism in those countries and the negative impact of global capitalism. He foretold the rise of fundamentalist movements that may eventually undermine democracy. Andre wrote 40 books and a thousand articles on these subjects.

The Folklorist

They called him the "Joke Professor". Few aspects of culture escaped his scrutiny. If people did it, said it, made it, wrote it or believed it **Alan Dundes** wanted to know why. He spent forty years as a professor at the University of California—Berkeley teaching anthropology and folklore. He studied contemporary culture and stories passed on from one person to another as well as the fables of the past. Alan became one of the most cited scholars in the world and was the first folklorist to be elected a member of the American Academy of Arts and Sciences. Among his other honors was an international lifetime achievement award in folklore and designation as a senior fellow of the National Endowment of the Humanities.

The Philosopher

He called his work an investigation into "the phenomenon of human life" and it ranged over a vast spectrum of human experience. The diverse subjects included myths and symbols, language, religion, ethics, the nature of evil and theories of literature and the law. **Paul Ricoeur** was one of the most eminent philosophers of the 20th century. He was best known for his work in phenomenology, the study of how the perception of events can shape a person's sense of reality. Paul explored the forces that underpin human action and suffering. He would take positions that appeared to be at opposite ends and work to see if there was a middle ground. In 2004 he shared the John Kluge Prize for Lifetime Achievement in the Human Sciences, an award that is described as a Nobel Prize for the humanities.

Essays Graded by a Computer

When he began his research in 1966, computers filled an entire room and were only being used to quickly compute complex math problems. The personal computer was still years away. **Ellis Page** had handwritten essays key punched into the mainframes. His program measured quantities that matched the basic qualities of sound writing habits that meet the approval of the average reader. When large words and long sentences were used, it indicated a command of a large vocabulary and the expression of a complex thought process. Ellis demonstrated that the computer scores did not differ significantly from those of human judges. He continued his work through the 1990's and a later version of his program is still in use today.

Advanced Computer Math

While a researcher at the Russian Academy of Sciences in Moscow in 1979, **Leonid Khachiyan** showed that certain problems in linear programming could be solved practically and in a reasonable amount of computing time. Computer scientists had previously relied on a method using a simple equation to review and order vast stores of information. In a scholarly paper, Leonid proposed using a new equation in the form of an algorithm which would address complex problems that could not be solved by the simple equation format. His algorithm received widespread approval and was refined for applications in finance, engineering and industry and helped to schedule complex rosters of airline flights.

Distance Learning

Recruited by the University of Southern California in 1968 to build up its engineering department, **Jack Munushian** knew firsthand the struggles that engineers had with getting advanced degrees in a college setting. Driving in heavy traffic after work made the goal difficult to achieve. Jack created the idea for the Instructional Television Network (ITV), a system in which classes could be broadcast on TV so industry professionals could attend classes more easily after work. By 1988 the school had recorded more than 50,000 enrollments. That same year Jack was given the highly coveted Major Educational Innovation Award by the Institute of Electrical Engineers. Jack's original concept would expand significantly with the growth of the Internet and the need for the availability of distance learning on a much greater scale with the time demands placed on the workforce.

Charter Schools

A charter school is a public school that operates independently of the district board of education. **Ray Budde** coined the term "charter" in the 1970's to describe a fresh arrangement to support innovative teachers within the public school system. He was never in favor of charter schools replacing public education. In Ray's eyes the charter school could give teachers increased responsibility over course work in exchange for a greater degree of accountability for student achievement results.

Medical Educator

Eugene Stead recognized that trained people who lacked a complete medical education could still perform many clinical services and valuable assistance to overworked doctors. He established a two-year program for physician assistants and two former Navy hospital corpsmen were the first graduates in 1965. There are now more than 100 programs to train physician assistants and 50,000 licensed practitioners who conduct tests, prescribe medication, order and interpret diagnostic tests and provide clinical care. Eugene was also known for his groundbreaking studies of cardiac catheterization and congestive heart failure. He was an early proponent of the role that computer analysis plays in medical practice and helped to develop a research database that evolved into the Duke University Clinical Research Institute which today keeps diagnostic and treatment data on more than 250,000 patients.

Aided Education Reform

Harold Stevenson was a psychologist who specialized in child development. Twice in the 1980's he produced surveys which showed the deficiencies of American education compared to their counterparts in Japan and Taiwan. The initial study in 1984 was the first large cross-cultural survey of school achievement in the early grades. It found that American pupils scored much lower because they were lacking in the discipline and commitment to learning that their Asian counterparts exhibited. The second study in 1987 found that math ability in American primary and high school students was among the lowest of any industrialized country. Harold's work was often cited during the national debate over education standards in the late 1980's and early 1990's.

Black History

He made it his mission to reconstruct African American history book by book, covering subjects that ranged from slavery to the black power movement and many other areas. **James Haskins** wrote more than 100 books, most of whom were targeted toward young readers. He wrote about sports and popular cultural personalities like Hank Aaron, Stevie Wonder and Bill Cosby to political figures like Martin Luther King and Adam Clayton Powell. His adult books included biographies of Scott Joplin, Lionel Hampton and Richard Pryor. His portrait of the legendary Harlem cabaret, "The Cotton Club" was the inspiration for a later movie of the same name. In 1969, James' "Diary of a Harlem Schoolteacher" was the first book written by a black educator on the decay of inner-city schools.

The Early College

It was a time when educators were scrambling to jump start education to keep up with the Russians. Initiatives ranged from courses that allowed students to do college-credit work while still in high school to experimental admissions of talented high school students direct into college. **Elizabeth Hall** believed that high school students in the 1960's were maturing faster than previous generations and wanted to offer them a greater challenge. She established Simon's Rock College in 1964 specifically for high school age students. Students who otherwise would have been in the last two years of high school instead took the first two years of college. As its first president, Elizabeth articulated its mission, supervised construction of the campus, recruited the faculty, developed the innovative curriculum and recruited the first students.

Giant Science Fair

INSPIRE was one of the greatest successes in NASA's outreach educational programs. **William Taylor** and an associate created INSPIRE in 1989 to stimulate in high school students an appreciation for science and technology and turned them into radio wave researchers. The project provided audio frequency radio kits to more than 1,700 students and other groups over the past 16 years. In 1992, students from almost 1,000 high schools set up a network of ground stations across the United States to record data from an experiment on a space shuttle mission.

Challenged Gifted Students

In 1969 an 8th grade student in the Baltimore school system had run out of options to take a math course that would challenge the exceptional ability for his age. **Julian Stanley** was a school psychologist who asked the student to take a series of tests that included the college level SAT. After testing several gifted students, Julian recognized that standardized testing was the best method to identify talented students. Ten years later the Center for Talented Youth was established at Johns Hopkins University for pre-high school students to pursue college-level courses on weekends and during summer sessions. Similar programs were also established at colleges in the US as well as Ireland and Spain. By 2005, these more than 200,000 students had benefited from the more challenging course work.

Excavated Troy

The ancient city that Homer immortalized in "The Illiad" was first discovered in the 1870's in Turkey. Its size was found to be much smaller than thought for the legendary Troy. After fifty years of excavation inactivity, **Manfred Korfmann,** starting in 1972, applied new technology to reveal a city that was much larger than originally found. The Turkish government permitted him in the late 1980's to significantly expand his dig. Each summer since, the project has fielded 200 to 300 archaeologists, graduate students and scientists from over 30 countries. They have since uncovered a city that is perhaps ten times as large as was previously estimated.

Head Start

Urie Bronfenbrenner believed that keeping the family intact was one of the most critical challenges facing society. For several decades he provided a strong voice to offset the forces that were threatening the family structure. As an advocate of a parent's involvement in their children's education, Urie was named to the federal panel in 1965 that created the Head Start program that has now served 20 million disadvantaged children and families since its founding. Subsequent studies have shown that children in the program have fewer adjustment problems and higher achievement levels. Urie emphasized that parents and children interacting together was the best method to create a family bond.

ENGINEERING

Crash Test Dummies

In the early 1950's **Samuel Alderson** started his own company and won a contract to develop a primitive dummy to test jet ejection seats. More than ten years later, Ralph Nader's book "Unsafe at Any Speed" outraged the car buying public and prompted the National Highway Traffic Safety Administration to begin buying Samuel's now better developed dummies to test seat belts, air bags and other devices to minimize death and injury in car crashes. By the late 1960's he produced the first dummy built specifically for automotive testing. It is estimated that almost 330,000 lives have been saved since 1960 due to safety feature improvements in cars. Samuel also created humanlike figures called medical phantoms that were used to measure exposure to radiation and made synthetic wounds that produced fake blood for use in military training exercises.

The Greatest Architect

He enrolled in the Harvard Graduate School of Design at the advanced age of 35 in 1941. **Philip Johnson** made up in productivity what he had missed out on with his late start. He became the first winner of the Pritzker Prize which was established in 1979 to honor an architect of international stature. A year earlier he had won the Gold Medal of the American Institute of Architects, the highest award the American profession bestows on any of its members. He made his mark arguing the importance of the aesthetic side of architecture and claimed he had no interest in buildings except as works of art. Among his efforts that are considered masterworks of the 20th century are the Glass House, a residential structure where Philip lived in Connecticut, the sculpture garden at the Museum of Modern Art, the pre-Columbian gallery at Dumbarton Oaks in Washington, DC, the Seagram Building and the present day Sony Building (formerly the AT&T Building) in New York City.

Ferry Boats

Armed with engineering and naval architecture degrees, **Philip Spaulding** set a course on his own in 1952 when opened a firm out of his home. In the years ahead he would design some of the world's largest ferryboats. He was best known for the two 440-foot jumbo class ferries he designed for the state of Washington. Built in 1972, they could carry 2,000 people and 188 cars. For 25 years they were the largest double-ended ferries in the world. In all, Philip designed dozens of ferries including a car and passenger ferry that was built in 1959 for use between Port Angeles and Victoria, British Columbia. It still is in operation today. In 1979 he was honored as one of the world's most innovative and inventive naval architects.

Metallurgy

Morris Cohen was instrumental in the modern development of materials science and engineering from its roots in metallurgy. His interest in metals began when he worked for his father's company that processed scrap and sold it to local newspapers for their printing presses. In a report many years later to the National Academy of Sciences in 1974, Morris outlined the foundation of materials science and charted its direction. His research into the structure of iron and steel contributed to the development of high strength steels and helped to establish the principles underlying the creation of all synthetic materials including metals, plastics, ceramics, polymers and also biomaterials that are used to make medical implants. In 1977, President Jimmy Carter presented Morris with the nation's highest scientific honor, the National Medal of Science, for his research on the hardening of steel. Ten years later he received Japan's highest science award, the first materials scientist so honored.

Hybrid Car

Congress passed the Clean Air Act in 1970 which required the development of a car engine within six years that would eliminate 90% of the pollution that was being emitted from automobiles. **Victor Wouk** formed Petro-Electric Motors with a partner to develop a hybrid, part-gas and part-electric, car for the Environmental Protection Agency which was encouraging innovative designs. Their demonstration vehicle was a modified 1972 Buick Skylark that featured a rotary engine and an electric motor. The car met the strictest emission standards, got 30 miles to the gallon and had a top speed of 85 miles per hour. Victor's hybrid was the only one in the government's program and, by early 1974, it was the sole surviving vehicle out of seven being considered. After undergoing the final EPA tests, he and his partner were told, without explanation, that it did not meet the specifications. It would be another 23 years before Toyota introduced their Prius in 1997 in Japan, the first gas-electric car to be sold in the consumer market.

Dr. Roller Coaster

His love of roller coasters went back to his teen years when he road the Coney Island Cyclone. **Richard Brown** would later play a role in the design of more than 100 amusement park rides including the Disney parks, Six Flags, Universal Studios and Knott's Berry Farm. In his basement in 1972, Richard built a model of a thrill ride that had caused injuries to several teenage girls. He determined where the problem was and, in the process, invented the industry of biomechanical testing of theme park rides. Richard made sure that new rides were not only exciting, but also safe. Although some safety experts used mannequins in the testing stage, Richard would personally get on a ride to evaluate its safety. He also was a pioneer in medicine when, in 1977, he developed new ways to monitor the central nervous system of a patient before and after surgery. Today, the practice he developed is common in any operation that involves an instrument touching the spine.

Earthquake Safety

For nearly thirty years he directed the Berkeley Seismological Laboratory in California which measures the earth's movements along the San Andreas Fault. **Bruce Bolt** examined changes in waves recorded by seismometers and was an early advocate of making digital recordings on tape for computer analysis. He translated his research into safer and sturdier bridges and buildings around the world. Bruce served as a consultant to the Alaska pipeline and the Aswan Dam in Egypt. He had a major influence on California earthquake safety laws and helped to create the state's mandatory system of hazards mapping. With his influence, laws were passed to provide requirements to demonstrate earthquake safety for private schools and hospitals and the need to disclose earthquake weakness to potential homebuyers.

Lunar Scoop

There were many unknowns about the moon prior to the first manned landing in 1969. Among the questions: what's the surface like? **Ronald Scott** was a civil engineer at the California Institute of Technology who designed a scoop that an unmanned craft used in 1967 to collect samples that were returned to earth to determine the strength, texture and structure of the soil on the moon. His work with NASA continued as a consultant on soil mechanics for the Apollo missions and the Viking trip to Mars in 1976. Ronald also studied how the earth's soil reacts during landslides and earthquakes and was elected to the National Academy of Engineering in the mid-1970's.

ENVIRONMENT

The Nurseryman

For 50 years **Allen Haskell**'s plant nursery attracted serious gardeners in search of rare plants and expert advice. Located on eight acres, the nursery was set among gardens, cobblestone walkways, rare trees and an 18th century house. The Massachusetts nursery included such rare specimens as a 250-year old American dogwood and a Chinese dove tree. A hosta collection and topiaries attracted people from around the world.

Helped Canadian Natives

Villagers would tell their stories on video to demonstrate their way of living to the Canadian government. Traveling by boat, dog sled and cross-country skis, **Anthony Williamson** researched the native use of renewable resources and the impact of resettlement on traditional life. He gathered data that created a template to evaluate the land claims of northern aboriginal people. Anthony also traveled the Labrador coast to assess the health of seal fisheries, whitefish and seal trout on the east coast of James Bay. He documented the concerns of the people there whose way of life was being impacted by mining projects and training flights by military jets. He applied the same techniques to foster community development in India and Southeast Asia.

Gardened With Native Plants

Sara Stein attended a lecture in 1991 on natural habitats. Influenced by the presentation, she decided to restore a pond she had drained at her home in New York state to encourage wildlife to return. Soon afterward she wrote 'Noah's Garden' which quickly became a reference book for natural habitat gardening. Sara emphasized the use of working with the local climate to nature's cycles that represented swamp, prairie, rock barren and other native environments and resulted in the return of birds, small mammals and other wildlife. Before her foray into gardening, Sara had written a series of books on how to raise various pets. In the mid-1970's she authored books that were intended to be read by both parents and children together and focused on such sensitive topics as hospitals, dying and handicaps.

The African Rhino

He first met a rhino at age 10 in a wild animal park near his home in England. His father remembered him very quickly warming to the rhino by scratching its nose and feeding it bananas. By age 20 **Mike Hearn** contacted the Save the Rhino International organization looking for a job in conservation. He moved up through the ranks and wound up spending 11 years in Namibia as director of the Save the Rhino Trust. Mike was at the forefront of setting up community-based conservation projects and used tourism as a means to fund them. He also made several films on the desert black rhino including a program featured on the BBC.

The Naturalist

They called her the Queen Bee. From her earliest youth **Miriam Rothschild** loved animals and plants and had no formal education until she was 17. Her interests ranged from marine biology to chemistry to pharmacology to neuro-physiology to horticulture to zoology. She often came up with novel and startling conclusions. Miriam was taken seriously as a scientist and often worked with dis-tinguished colleagues. Her well-known work on butterflies was done with a Nobel Prize winning chemist. She established the modern "web-of-life" view of conservation which looks upon the protection of the habitat as the vital element in the survival of threatened species. Miriam received 8 honorary doctorates and a fellowship in the Royal Society.

Witches Brooms

With America transitioning into tract housing in the years after World War II, there was a demand for trees and shrubs that would fit into small yards and would not grow very much. **Sidney Waxman** would travel to the New England area in the fall to get the seeds from witch's brooms, a clump of large branches on full sized pine trees. The branches held cones whose seedlings would produce dwarf evergreens for the front lawns of suburbia. Over 40 years Sidney had raised 200,000 seedlings to get 40 cultivated plant varieties. He would plant the cones at a nursery at the University of Connecticut to see what the next generation of mutations would look like. If he liked what he saw he made clippings and sent them to nurseries around the United States.

Greenpeace

Bob Hunter was bent on changing the world with "media mindbombs" that would alter people's opinions by sounds and images in the form of news. He got involved with a few people who wanted to stop a US nuclear weapons test off the coast of Alaska in 1971. As a columnist for the Vancouver Sun newspaper he thought he was going as a reporter to take a few notes and wound up staying on their small fishing boat for 45 days. Bob called their protest "Don't Make a Wave" and it was the first action that established the environmental group called Greenpeace. He became its first president in 1973 and led it through its transformation into an international group that now has more than 2.5 million members worldwide in 40 countries. In 2000 Time magazine named Bob as one of the 20th century's top 10 environmental heroes.

Caring for Citrus

Homer Chapman made substantial contributions to citrus nutrition and soil research. It was his work that that added to the economic growth of the citrus industry in California and around the world. He was a pioneer in the development of leaf and tissue analysis for diagnosing the nutrient status of citrus trees. Homer's methods of evaluating soils are still in use today. He worked on other issues related to the citrus culture, such as pest management. Other citrus growing areas adopted what was learned through his research. His five volume "Citrus Industry" is considered the bible for the industry and citrus researchers.

British Ecologist

The most influential naturalist of his generation. **Derek Ratcliffe** earned that distinction with his mastery of a broad range of subjects. He was an expert bird observer, accomplished plant ecologist and a trendsetter in describing and classifying wild vegetation. Through his research he discovered that DDT was thinning eggshells and paved the way for the ban of its use within the European Union. In the 1960's and 70's he developed a keen sense of the changing face of the countryside and established a framework for the conservation of nature. Derek seized the opportunity to lead the production of an inventory of Britain's best sites for wildlife and habitats.

Fought Against the Threat of Chemicals

The "precautionary principle" formed his view on how to react to the perils caused by chemicals. **Marc Lappe** believed that if the risk is high and the outcome is unknown, it's best to avoid introducing the risk altogether. Marc also felt that even a slight risk could be a concern and that long-term exposure to very low doses might become dangerous. He was a consultant or witness in cases involving industrial waste, Agent Orange, farm workers' exposure to pesticides and the effects of pollution. His books were among the first to raise questions about the rapid increase in chemicals in modern life, the widespread use of antibiotics and genetically altered crops. Marc founded the Center for Ethics and Toxics to help local communities fight contamination.

Global Warming

Carbon dioxide traps heat in the atmosphere. Scientists did not think that emissions from cars and factories could have an impact on the earth's climate, they thought that plants or the oceans would absorb it. In 1958 **Charles Keeling** established a base two miles high on Mauna Loa volcano in Hawaii to measure daily gas levels. His measurements found that the concentration of carbon dioxide had been rising steadily since the onset of the Industrial Age. He linked the increase to emissions from factories and cars around the world. Charles showed that the levels rise and fall with the seasons and follow the cycle of vegetation in the northern hemisphere. In later years he found that the seasonal swings have become greater. In 2002 he was awarded the National Medal of Science by President Bush and in 2005 received the Tyler Prize for Environmental Achievement, the most prestigious award for environmental research.

Earth Day

Gaylord Nelson was a US Senator from Wisconsin who had just finished visiting an oil spill off the coast of Santa Barbara, California in 1969. On his return trip he decided that something needed to be done to raise awareness about the declining state of the environment. The first Earth Day on April 22, 1970 attracted an estimated 20 Million Americans who helped to clean creeks, recycle tin cans and basically assist in trying to improve the environment. Earth Day started what came to be called the decade of the environment in which 28 major laws were passed in the 1970's, many of which Gaylord had a hand in. He was considered one of the leading environmentalists of the 20th century and co-sponsored the Wilderness Act and laws that protected the Appalachian Trail and banning the pesticide DDT. In 1995 he was awarded the Presidential Medal of Freedom by President Bill Clinton.

Solo Across the Atlantic

The French have always been known to be adventuresome. They were the first to cross Niagara Falls on a tightrope, walk from Paris to Moscow on stilts and row across the Pacific Ocean. **Alain Bombard** had been inspired by Thor Heyerdahl's 1947 crossing of the oceans on a rudimentary raft. Alain wanted to take the challenge a step farther to see if a person could survive an ocean journey without supplies of fresh water and provisions. He set out alone in Monaco and made his way to Barbados in 65 days. He encountered both storms and weeks of very calm seas and nearly drowned six times. Alain was a medical doctor and subsisted on plankton, saltwater and raw fish. He made the trip in a fifteen foot inflatable dinghy equipped with a compass, fishing gear, a nylon filter, a few books, a pair of oars and a single sail.

Location Analysis

It began as an emerging field in the 1960's. Location analysis considers an array of variables in finding a site for a given project such as a reservoir or a hospital and then tries to plug in those variables into a math model known as an algorithm. The model yields a solution that suggests the most effective and environmentally sound site for a facility. **Charles ReVelle** applied his algorithms to a sweeping set of subjects that grew to include the location and optimal scale of warehouses, emergency services, treatment plants and efficient routes for transportation and power grids. Charles' models were also extended into other areas such as helping the city of Baltimore in the 1970's determine which surplus fire stations to close and finding the balance between cost effective timber harvesting while protecting delicate forest species.

Defending the Environment

Plans were made in the early 1970's to develop the Mineral King Valley in the Sierra Nevada mountains. The Environmental Policy Act had recently been put into law so **Fred Fisher** and a partner volunteered to help the Sierra Club fight the development project. The proposed ski resort was not built and, out of their efforts, the Sierra Club legal defense fund was formed to provide free legal representation to protect the environment. Over the past 35 years the fund has offered their services to more than 600 clients, both large and small, including the National Audubon Society and Friends of the Everglades, and have been involved in cases centering on public lands, national forests, wilderness areas, pollution and wildlife habitat. The fund was renamed Earthjustice in 1997 and now has a staff of 140 with an annual budget of $30 million.

Philadelphia Flower Show

It's origins dated to 1829, but by the early 1960's there was talk of suspending for two years the annual flower show in Philadelphia. **Ernesta Drinker Ballard** became the executive director of the Pennsylvania Horticultural Society in 1963 and would eventually turn the society's flower show into the largest indoor flower show in the United States, drawing today more than 250,000 people a year. She directed the show until 1981 and opened it to amateur growers and used it as a teaching laboratory for a wider audience. In time the show began to turn a surplus. With that money Ernesta began a community gardening program, Philadelphia Green, which turned vacant lots into vegetable gardens and flowerbeds and became one of the largest urban greening projects in the country.

Giraffe Manor

A Rothschild giraffe has white legs and five horns and numbered about 120 in the early 1970's. **Betty Leslie-Melville** called herself "a total giraffe junkie" and helped to save the breed from extinction by taking a patch of land in Kenya and turning it into a sanctuary of 18,000 acres as a natural habitat. Today the breed now numbers close to 500 throughout Africa. She and her husband were the only people known to have raised wild giraffe. After her husband died in 1984, Betty opened their house to visitors and it was given the name Giraffe Manor. It was common for a giraffe to poke its nose into the windows of upper-floor guest rooms.

MEDICINE

Pediatrician Until Age 95

In the 1960's **Sol Londe** first began developing methods to measure blood pressure in children. His work holds even more relevance today with the high increase in childhood obesity. Sol's research also moved into the area of childhood hypertension. By the time he had retired from private practice, he moved to Los Angeles in his 70's and joined the volunteer faculty at UCLA medical school. In his 80's he worked as a doctor in a juvenile hall detention center and did not stop practicing medicine until his license expired at the age of 95. In the early 1980's Sol founded the LA chapter of Physicians for Social Responsibility, an organization that won the Nobel Prize in 1985.

Medic Alert

Linda Maurer cut her finger as a child and went into shock at the hospital from an allergic reaction. Her father was a doctor and he asked Linda to wear a bracelet with a note attached that explained her medical condition. Her parents recognized that the problem extended beyond Linda and started the Medic Alert Foundation out of their garage in 1956. It would grow to include 4 million worldwide members and save about 4,000 lives each year. Linda continued to wear a bracelet throughout her life. Her original bracelet is in the Smithsonian Institute in Washington, DC.

Vaccine Expert

While in grade school he was awed by his brother's Gilbert chemistry set. At age 10 he read an article in Look magazine about a doctor who worked with vaccines. **John La Montague** was hooked and decided to make it his life's work. He was trained as a microbiologist and worked with scientists in more than 100 countries to find cures for diseases. He spent nearly 30 years at the National Institute of Allergy and Infectious Diseases and conducted research on influenza, AIDS, whooping cough, child pneumonia and malaria. Among his many awards was the Surgeon General's Certificate of Appreciation.

Brought Antibiotics Outside the Lab

Jasper Kane started out as a teenage assistant at the Charles Pfizer plant where he learned to ferment sugar. Later on Jasper developed a deep-tank fermentation process that used molasses in place of refined sugar. Up to that time penicillin was being made dose by dose. With the onset of the United States' entry into World War II, hundreds of soldiers were dying daily. His deep-tank method was able to make penicillin and other antibiotics in mass quantities for the first time. By the end of 1943 the plant was making 45 million units of broad-spectrum antibiotics. In the 1950's Jasper was credited with leading the team that developed the synthetic antibiotic Terramycin which is still in use today.

Neurosurgeon Worked with Epilepsy

Epilepsy is a disorder caused by the abnormal discharge of the brain's nerve cells and can cause seizures and loss of memory and control of the body. A typical surgical procedure was to put the patient under local anesthesia during the operation, but it was met with inconsistent results. **Sidney Goldring** introduced a procedure in the 1970's to put electrodes on the brain under general anesthesia to locate the affected area of the brain and cut out the diseased tissue while the patient was still awake. The technique allowed the practice to be used on children. Sidney served as president of the American Academy of Neurological Surgery.

Healing Waters

Following the revolution in Iran in 1979, **Fereydoon Batmanghelidj** was imprisoned for nearly three years. A practicing physician, he treated fellow prisoners for ulcers and severe abdominal pain by recommending that they drink a large amount of water to ward off their dehydration. After being released he moved to the United States and began lecturing and presenting scientific papers based on the premise that most pain and sickness is the result of chronic dehydration of the body. Fereydoon was faced with people critical of his belief, but a self-help book he published in 1992 was translated into 15 languages.

Cardiologist

In the 1940's **M. Irene Ferrer** was a doctor working at Bellevue Hospital in New York City and participated in groundbreaking research that led to the catheter, a flexible tube that is passed through the veins and directly into the heart or coronary arteries. It allows a precise measurement of blood pressure and blood flow and has made possible the use of angioplasty and other revolutionary heart treatments. Two other members of the team won the Nobel Prize in 1956 for this work. M. Irene went on to help refine the EKG machine which records the beat of the heart. She created a computer-assisted algorithm that permits a clearer and quicker reading. This was a significant improvement from the earlier method in which only doctors with specialized training could interpret the results.

Neonatologist

William Silverman was the director of the newborn intensive care unit at Babies Hospital of Columbia-Presbyterian in the 1950's. At the time it was common for doctors to use excessive oxygen to treat newborns. The result was thousands of babies that were blinded from a minor change in caretaking. William's work validated that the problems were being caused by too much oxygen. The practice was changed and significantly fewer infants became blinded. Also during that time period there was a rapid increase in the number of interventions and medications that were introduced to treat newborns. William analyzed their side effects to keep treatment in check for the child's benefit. In 2003 he received the Migel Medal from the American Foundation for the Blind, their highest honor.

Ophthalmologist

In 1999, **J. Donald M. Gass** was named one of the ten most influential ophthalmologists of the 20th century by a professional eye surgery society. What was most impressive was that while he was at the Bascom Palmer Eye Institute at the University of Miami in the 1970's, he wrote a groundbreaking book on retinal diseases that described several hundred eye diseases. While researching his book, Dr. Gass helped to pioneer a test that traces a vegetable dye injected into blood vessels within the retina that reveals signature patterns of leaking and blockage with the vessels. He was also able to describe the causes of macular holes and several other macular disorders.

Heart Surgery and the Pacemaker

Wilfred Bigelow was stationed at a hospital in England during World War II and noticed that low temperatures reduced the need for oxygen in soldiers with frostbitten limbs. He and an engineer built a device that could cool the extremities while allowing the limbs to warm more slowly to minimize damage. A few years later, it came to Wilfred in the middle of the night that the entire body could be cooled to temporarily stop the heart during surgery. Other physicians thought it would be a death sentence for a patient. In 1949 the technique was first used successfully on a dog and three years later it was used on a human. By the 1960's, the heart-lung machine took the lead and is now combined, to a lesser extent, with Wilfred's technique. During his studies of hypothermia in 1950, he found that an electrical impulse to the heart would stimulate a beat. Again with the assistance of an engineer, he created a radio-sized unit that could restart a patient's heart after it cooled. It took the introduction of the transistor nearly ten years later to begin implants in humans.

The Neurologist

Christopher Pallis was probably the best-known neurological teacher of his time due to his extensive training of other neurologists throughout the world. His intellect, command of logic and charismatic enthusiasm made him an outstanding clinician. He traveled widely, especially in Asia, to study tropical diseases of the nervous system. Christopher's concept of, and criteria for, brainstem death have been internationally adopted. His article on death for the Encyclopedia Britannica is considered a masterpiece of historical and medical summary.

Fabric Safety

Working in an era before cosmetic surgery was commonplace, **George Crikelair** was a reconstructive surgeon who operated on everything from the top of the head to the bottom of the feet. In the late 1950's he had noticed a pattern among child patients who had severe injuries from burned clothing, often untreated cotton sleepwear. He was named to a national advisory committee that helped to draft and promote a federal law in 1972 that set safety standards for certain fabrics. Through George's influence many potential burn victims were saved.

Hematologist

He was described as one of the top hematologists in the United States in the 1950's and 1960's. Any experiment he performed he also performed on himself. **William Crosby** invented one of the first devices to obtain a biopsy of the bowel. It became useful to doctors because it provided a nonsurgical way to take out tissue and contributed to a better understanding of the link between a bowl disorder and a type of anemia. William also studied a broad range of topics that included the effects of nutrition in producing anemia and other blood disorders, damage from too much or too little iron in the body and the functions of the bone marrow and the spleen. He also examined ways to save lives by restoring the proper amounts of blood and fluids to victims of war injuries and accidents.

Pediatric Neurology

When he arrived at Columbia University in 1947, **Sidney Carter** noticed that specialists for children were uncommon at hospitals. So he set out to establish training programs and certifications for neurologists to diagnose and treat diseases among children. In the 1950's Sidney and others persuaded the National Institute of Health to support training fellowships specifically designed for pediatric neurology which created guidelines for neurology residents to study multiple sclerosis in children, optic neuritis and other disorders. He was chosen president of the American Academy of Neurology in 1969 and nine years later he became president of the American Neurological Association.

Hypertension Expert

Edward Freis was working at the Veterans Administration Hospital in Washington in the 1960's when he and his colleagues conducted a five year study of patients with high blood pressure. It was widely believed at the time that high blood pressure was helpful in circulating blood to the brain and should not be treated. Half received placebos and the other half were treated with medication that formed urine in the kidneys. The placebo group had serious health problems while the medicated group only had one event. The striking contrast of the study helped to establish the benefits of treating and reducing hypertension. At the end of the study they determined that drug treatment cut deaths from moderate hypertension by half and reduced strokes by two-thirds. For his work Edward received the Albert Lasker Award for clinical medical research in 1971 for demonstrating the potential of preventive medicine.

Hand Surgeon

J. William Littler was a young surgeon in the Army during World War II. Although he had not yet completed his residency training, his work on maimed soliders shaped and refined surgical techniques that are still in use today. He worked on new ways to reconstruct missing thumbs, including replacing them with parts of forefingers, and he transplanted healthy bundles of nerves and arteries to areas that had lost feeling. In order to revive arms and hands paralyzed by nerve damage, he transferred tendons from areas that were unharmed. In the 1950's he founded the hand surgery unit at the hospital now known as St.

Luke's-Roosevelt and trained hundreds of surgeons. The unit was the first to devote itself to civilian hand injuries.

Broadened Psychoanalysis

Phyllis Meadow believed that any qualified person with a college degree should be able to pursue training in psychoanalysis without having a medical degree. The regulatory body in the field did not initially see it the same way. With a doctorate in human relations, Phyllis set as her objectives the need to create greater diversity among the types of patients that are treated and reduce the number of therapeutic sessions from 3 to 5 a week down to one or two. By 1988, the American Psychoanalytic Association agreed to open training to candidates without medical degrees. Phyllis also lobbied successfully to liberalize training by getting the federal law changed as well as new laws in several states including California and New York.

Child Abuse

While attending a meeting of the American Academy of Pediatrics in 1961, **Brandt Steele** joined a panel that raised the awareness of the problem of child abuse. The following year Brandt and an associate released a paper that became the first to detail the symptoms of child abuse by parents. They called it "battered child syndrome" and the frequently used term "battered child" was coined from their paper. The Journal of the American Medical Association called the paper one of the 20th century's 50 most important medical contributions. Brandt found that abusive parents had usually been badly treated themselves and they were often reflexively repeating the violence as an adult. He was instrumental in the development of the National Center for the Prevention and Treatment of Child Abuse and neglect. Brandt also went on to write extensively about infanticide, sexual abuse and the detection and treatment of abusive parents.

Heart Catheter

Jeremy Swan joined the Cedars-Sinai Medical Center in 1965 as chief of cardiology. At the time it was not understood what effective procedure was needed to help a patient after they had a heart attack except to treat the complications caused by it. In the late 60's the cardiology department received a sizable grant from the National Institute of Health to improve the knowledge and treatment of heart attacks. Jeremy knew that not all heart attacks are caused by the same problem and should not receive a uniform treatment. By 1970 he and a colleague invented the heart catheter which measures the characteristics of a heart attack and allows a more precise diagnosis and treatment. Since its invention it has been used on millions of patients.

Surgery on a Submarine

It was the middle of World War II and the submarine was a week away from the nearest friendly port. A seaman was suffering from appendicitis and no one on board was a doctor. **Wheeler Lipes** was 22 and a pharmacist's mate on the sub. He had previously observed several appendectomies as a lab technician at a navy hospital. With the sick seaman's permission, a team was put together, led by Wheeler, to perform the operation. A tea strainer covered with gauze became an ether mask. Metal spoons bent at right angles served as muscle retractors to hold the wound open. Boiled water and alcohol sterilized the instruments. Wheeler removed the appendix after two and a half hours in the first appendectomy ever performed on board a submerged submarine. The patient returned to duty in a timely fashion. The surgery was later dramatized in two Hollywood movies and a television series. It was not until February 2005 that the Navy recognized Wheeler's deed when he received a Commendation Medal.

Child Psychiatry

Until the 1960's, children with a wide range of developmental disabilities and behavior problems were largely ignored by mainstream psychiatry. Children with severe emotional disturbances who needed hospitalization had no choice and were treated in adult programs. **James Simmons** established a program at UCLA in 1962 that promoted a more humane service for children who were diagnosed as mentally retarded or autistic and established one of the first training programs for professionals who would work with the children. James devised methods that allowed more children with autism to live at home and attend school. Those methods formed the mainstay of behavioral treatment for autism today.

Breast Cancer Research

She was called the ultimate patient advocate. **Jeanne Petrek** became one of the first doctors to take an interest in a cancer patient's long-term quality of life. She was a leading expert on pregnancy-associated breast cancer. In her 20 years at the Memorial-Sloan Kettering Cancer Center in New York City, Jeanne treated more than 4,000 women and sought ways to give them a better life after cancer surgery. She conducted the first ever-extensive study of the safety of pregnancy for women who had suffered from breast cancer. She was nearing the conclusion of a ten-year study on the changes in ovary function that resulted from cancer treatment and was following the histories of 800 women under age 44 who had undergone chemotherapy.

Open Heart Surgery

In 1952, **William Cleland** headed up a group of colleagues from Hammersmith Hospital in London who traveled to the Soviet Union to demonstrate the use of a heart-lung machine to 200 Soviet surgeons. The group returned to London only with their luggage, the six operations they performed were such a success that all of their equipment was purchased by the Soviets. The following year William and two other physicians performed the first successful open-heart operation in Great Britain.

Medical Anthropology

While teaching at Harvard, **Benjamin Paul** published in 1955 a landmark case study of public reactions to health programs that is still in use today. Evaluating medical conditions in China, Puerto Rico and Peru, he came to the conclusion that international aid programs had to closely consider local cultural beliefs in order to be effective. He felt that people's behavior makes sense if you understand it from their own view of the world. For this work Benjamin is considered to be the founding father of medical anthropology, which applies questions about health and healing. He was also closely involved with conducting fieldwork in South America on sanitation and fluoridation. In 1994 Benjamin received the distinguished service award from the American Anthropological Association.

Joint Surgeon

It was estimated that **Hugh Phillips** performed more than 6,000 joint replacement operations in his career. His early experience in knee replacements of only the surface of the destroyed joint made him a sought after trainer of young surgeons. In 1990 he was voted England's surgical trainer of the year. Hugh was proficient in working on ankle and hip joints and was an innovator of the surgery in the late 1970's and early 1980's. He had a particular expertise in replacing joints destroyed by arthritis. As the founder of the British Hip Society, Hugh helped establish the National Joint Registry, which records every major joint replacement operation in the country. He was elected President of the Royal College of Surgeons in 2004.

Open Heart Surgery

Clarence Dennis first began his research into the heart-lung machine in the late 1930's at the University of Minnesota. The dangers of repairing a damaged heart had severely limited the interest of surgeons in prior years. Nearly a decade later he led a team that obtained federal funding to pursue development of the machine. By 1951 Clarence was performing the first open heart surgery that used a heart-lung bypass machine. Although the surgery was not successful, the groundwork had been laid for further progress. A few years later he became the second surgeon in the country to perform open-heart surgery that involved a mechanical pump oxygenator. This surgery was a success. By the 1970's Laurence had joined the National Institute of Health in their medical device application program which was aimed at developing artificial hearts. Throughout his career he invented and patented surgical instruments, including two that bear his name.

The Link to Smoking

In the first half of the 20th century smoking was considered too normal to be dangerous. However, studies in the 1930's by German and Dutch doctors were beginning to show a link between smoking and lung cancer. They did not draw wide attention because they were not published in English. **Richard Doll** released a study, with an associate, in 1950 that was considered to be the first worldwide official report on the dangers of tobacco. A survey of lung cancer patients in London hospitals and a later larger survey of 34,000 doctors over a twenty-year period established a firm link between cigarettes and lung cancer. Queen Elizabeth knighted Richard in 1971 for his contributions to public health. In separate studies he also showed that small doses of radiation could also cause cancer.

Nuclear Medicine

As a key member of a University of Chicago research team, **Paul Harper** was one of the first to investigate several of the tools of modern nuclear medicine. In the 1960's they introduced a radioactive element into a patient's bloodstream and traced its progress through the brain, heart, liver and other organs. The substance is now used nearly 35,000 times a day in the United States and 20 million times a year worldwide to identify tumors or unusual physical processes. The team became leaders in the use of various types of radioactive implants to deliver a therapeutic dose to tumors that is now routine for prostate cancer. Paul found ways to apply it to other sites throughout the body including the pancreas and brain. The process is able to shrink or destroy cancers and tumors.

Blood Banks

The practice of a patient donating and storing their own blood was known for more than a century, but was not implemented on a wide scale until **Margot Kruskall** established such a program in Boston stemming from concerns about hepatitis infections. The timing was well received as the spread of AIDS in the1980's was becoming more common. Margot and others at Beth Israel Hospital set up a system to label the blood, decided what surgical procedures were best served by it and created an inventory system. Their work inspired similar programs in other parts of the country. Margot's more recent work involved research to develop a universal red blood cell that could be safely infused, regardless of a patient's blood type.

The Rheumatoid Factor

Initial discoveries of a signature antibody in the bloodstream of arthritis patients first took place in the 1930's. By the 50's and 60's **Morris Ziff** was able to trace the source of the antibody to joints inflamed by arthritis. The rheumatoid factor was developed as a blood test and has become a leading method to diagnose the disease. Later on, Morris became a co-discoverer of other markers in the bloodstream of damage to the joints caused by rheumatic fever and other diseases. During his career he trained 120 physicians in rheumatology who went on to positions of responsibility around the world.

Mother's Little Helper

When he tried it he said it made him drowsy. The drug became a cultural symbol in books and movies for the frenzied life of the modern age. **Leo Sternbach** created Valium almost by accident. After initial work on it in the 1950's he had put it aside for more than a year until a technician wanted to throw it away. He revisited its effects and the pill was released under the name Librium, a predecessor to the more potent and popular Valium which Leo synthesized from Librium. Introduced in 1963, Valium became the most common prescription drug in America between 1969 and 1982. At its peak in 1978, over 2 billion pills were sold. It was immortalized in the Rolling Stones hit record 'Mother's Little Helper' in 1967. In all, Leo was credited with 241 drug patents. He was named by U.S. News & World Report as one of the 25 most influential Americans of the 20th century and was also inducted into the National Inventors Hall of Fame.

SCIENCE

Studied the Planets

His interests ranged from Venus, Jupiter and Saturn to the Moon and Earth. **Thomas Donahue** began by studying cosmic rays from space and the effects of radiation on the atmosphere of the Earth and other planets. He then became an advocate of using satellites and spacecraft for his observations. Thomas led the group for the Pioneer missions to Venus in the 1970's and was involved in the Voyager, Galileo and Cassini trips to the outer planets as well as working on the studies of the destruction of the protective ozone layers in the Earth's stratosphere. By 1983 he was elected to the National Academy of Sciences.

Pioneer Female Physicist

She received a doctorate in physics from the University of California at Berkley in 1933 during a time when very few women received any type of advanced degree. Together with her mentor, the renowned J. Robert Openheimer, they offered an explanation of heavy hydrogen atoms that became a classic of early nuclear physics. **Melba Phillips** went on to develop and implement training for physics teaching at all grade levels and led a movement to improve physics teacher preparation. By the mid 1960's she had become the first woman president of the American Association of Physics Teachers. In 2003 she was given the Joseph Burton Forum award by the American Physical Society for being "a model of a principled scientist".

Prostglandins

His first laboratory was a shed built by his father in the family garden. **John Vane** had already caused explosions with a chemistry set his father had given to him and his father was unwilling to take any further chances in the house. Prostglandins are natural compounds from fatty acids that control many bodily functions. They were first identified in the 1930's, but were not well understood. In the 1960's, John was able to determine the precise makeup of some prostglandins. With his discovery, new treatments were created for high blood pressure, heart failure and controlling pulmonary hypertension. He shared the Nobel Prize for Medicine in 1982 and was knighted in Great Britain two years later.

The Genome

Isidore Edelman began as a physiology researcher at Harvard studying how the body distributes its essential salts and minerals that are known as electrolytes and carried through the body as blood and body fluids. Isidore used radioactive material to trace their route in the body and bloodstream. Later on at the University of California, San Francisco, he observed a hormone's effect on the ability of a kidney to absorb salt. Additional work addressed the thyroid hormone function and its role in producing body heat. By 1978 he had joined Columbia University and fifteen years later became co-director of their Human Genome Program.

Radiation Standards

A career of 50 years began at the National Bureau of Standards in 1927. **Lauriston Taylor** led a number of organizations that set radiation exposure guidelines for workers and the public. He wrote more than 150 scientific papers and part or all of 16 books. Early on he built instruments to measure X-rays and calibrate other devices and was credited as being the first person to build a portable radiation survey meter. He was a delegate to several significant international conferences and was considered as one of the leading scientists in radiation health protection in the 20th century.

The Nutritionist

The thought of using human beings for nutrition testing was never considered until **Sheldon Margen** began doing it in the mid-1950's. His research became the foundation for the 1977 US dietary guidelines that were the first government recommendations on diet and its effect on disease. Those findings also form the basis for diet guidelines listed today on packaged food. Sheldon's research became accepted doctrine on calcium and bone metabolism, protein, energy needs and obesity. The 'Wellness Letter' was launched in 1984 to offer practical advice about staying healthy at a time when there was a limited amount of health information available. The subscriber list now totals 300,000.

The Nobel Chemist

His father died when he was 14 and **Herbert Brown** dropped out of school for a while to help run the family business. He returned to earn a doctorate from the

University of Chicago in 1938. Herbert pursued a career in chemistry and created more than 50 combinations of boron and hydrogen that were versatile in manufacturing drugs and other difficult to make organic compounds. For these efforts he shared the 1979 Nobel Prize in chemistry. His work revolutionized many areas of chemistry by significantly reducing the time to synthesize new compounds for drug testing. Those compounds have contributed to the effective manufacturing process for hydrocortisone, steroids and prostaglandins, all of which are now widely used to treat illness.

Innovator in Radiation

It didn't take long for **John Laughlin** to become proactive when he joined Memorial Hospital (the forerunner of Sloan-Kettering) in New York City in 1952. He helped to acquire their first betatron machine that was used to point a stream of high-energy electrons at cancerous tumors to shrink or destroy them. During that same time period he conducted research into how radiation could be used to make better medical diagnoses. He brought in a cyclotron machine that was used to produce radioactive isotopes that could be injected and then traced through the bloodstream. In later years John moved into a field known as dosimetry and addressed the dangers of radiation by determining the extent of the exposure to radiation by medical workers, scientists and the public.

The Nature of Brain Cells

In the late 1930's **Julius Axelrod** was testing the potency of vitamins added to food when a bottle of ammonia exploded and blinded him in his left eye. His commitment to research never wavered as he won the Nobel Prize in Medicine in 1970 for his work in the development of psychiatric drugs such as Prozac, Paxil and Zoloft. Most scientists had believed that chemicals in the brain became inactive when enzymes broke them down, but Julius' work showed that they were actually pumped back into the nerve cells that had released them. Those chemicals help to regulate digestion, heartbeat and blood flow. It was only a few years after his injury that he helped to identify acetaminophen as the pain-relieving chemical in a common headache treatment of the time. The substance was commercially developed and sold under the brand name Tylenol.

Genetic Researcher

When in college he scored so well on a nationally administered science test that he was asked to retake it. **Rollin Hotchkiss** began work in the 1940's concentrating on bacteria that causes pneumonia. The studies ultimately led to the concept of genetic transformation and explained the biochemical basis of heredity by showing that hereditary material in an organism is passed through DNA and not through proteins as was originally believed. Rollin was elected to the American Academy of Sciences in 1958 and the National Academy of Sciences in 1961.

The Study of Blood

John Dacie began studying hemolytic anemia in the mid 1930's in England. It is a condition that occurs when the bone marrow can't increase the production of red blood cells to compensate for the destruction of other red cells. He devoted his professional life to the disease. He was known as a great laboratory scientist who would leave clinical work to his colleagues. Students from around the world would come to England to work with him and return to their home countries to become leading blood experts. The foremost leukemia research center in Great Britain was founded in 1969 and headed up by John for many years. It offers transplants of bone marrow which is responsible for the formation of blood cells. John was knighted in 1976.

Lassa Virus

In 1969 three missionary nurses in Nigeria quickly became sick and died from an unknown virus. A third nurse was evacuated to New York City where **Sonja Buckley**, a member of Yale University's virus research unit, began to study the virus by using samples of the nurse's blood. With assistance, Sonja was able to identify the virus by isolating tissue cultures. The virus was named after the village in Nigeria called Lassa where it was contracted. Her work showed that antibodies taken from survivors of the virus could be used in treatment.

Studied the Power of the Sun

For 60 years he used only a slide rule, a stack of blank paper and his prodigious intellect to crank out mistake-free complex calculations that changed how scientists viewed the atom. **Hans Bethe** fled to the United States to escape Nazi Germany in the 1930's. In a 1938 paper he explained one of the ways in which the sun fuses hydrogen into helium, releasing bursts of energy which results in light. The paper helped to establish his reputation as the father of nuclear astrophysics and earned him the Nobel Prize in 1967. Most of the 300 scientific papers he published in his career were originally classified as secret due to the implications of his findings. In order to defeat the Nazis Hans agreed to become a participant in the creation of the atomic bomb. However, after two were detonated to end World War II he spent the rest of his life becoming a very outspoken proponent of disarmament.

Treated Type I Diabetes

People who suffer from Type I diabetes have nonfunctioning "islet cells" that can't produce insulin. In 1967 **Paul Lacy** found a way to isolate and preserve beta cells. After years of experimentation on animals the first successful cell transplant test on a human was completed in 1989. Two years later Paul and a colleague were able to report that five transplant patients were insulin-independent. Once under the skin the islet cells act the same way as insulin producing cells in the pancreas. When the glucose goes up they hold the blood sugar at normal levels. The therapy continues as experimental and has yet to be approved by the Food and Drug Administration. In 1970 Paul also created the Juvenile Diabetes Foundation and worked diligently to raise money and attract young medical people to diabetes research.

DNA Research

It was called the pivotal discovery of 20th century biology. DNA had first been identified in the 19th century, but most scientists believed that it lacked the needed complexity to carry hereditary information. **Maclyn McCarty** was a member of a trio of researchers in the 1940's that were the first to firmly establish that genes were made of DNA. Their findings paved the way for molecular biology and genetic engineering. Because they were not self-promoters, the discovery received little publicity until Watson and Crick announced in 1953 the double helix structure of DNA, a watershed moment in science. In 1994 Maclyn did receive a Special Achievement in Medical Science award from the Lasker Foundation. The award is considered as the American equivalent of the Nobel Prize.

Evolutionary Biologist

The Darwin of the 20th century, defender of the faith. **Ernst Mayer** created the first working definition of what a species is and showed how genetics and population movements combined to create a new species, a process known as "modern synthesis" that was termed by an eminent biologist as one of the six major scientific achievements of the century. From his studies of birds in the South Pacific from 1928 to 1930, Ernst noticed that individual species of birds tend to occur in small geographic pockets that are separated from a closely related species that has slightly different genetic traits. He believed that over long periods of time a new species emerges in isolation. The small genetic changes accumulate rapidly and lead to the development of a new species that is no longer capable of breeding with the species they once were. His argument for the role of geography in the origin of a new species won universal acceptance among evolutionary theorists. Ernst also established a philosophy of biology and founded the field of the history of biology. He received 17 honorary degrees from nine countries.

The Science of Water

His driving ambition was to improve food production. **Charles Pereira** pioneered the study of the science of water and its relation to crops in tropical and temperate regions. Hydrology is a science that needs careful and precise measurements to confirm or deny myths about the effects of water on plants. Charles conducted his research nearly 20 years before hydrology became a respected science. He traveled to Africa in the mid-1940's to conduct field experiments and his work established new techniques to measure the effect that planting crops has on available water resources.

Bipolar Disorder

Peter Stokes began training in psychiatry during the 1960's at Cornell University where he taught for four decades. While at the Payne Whitney Clinic in 1965 he and other scientists began to investigate the effects of lithium in controlling bipolar disease and manic depression. They used lithium in the form of a salt to judge its effects. In 1970 lithium was approved for use in the United States and a year later the scientists' encouraging results were published in a British medical journal. Peter's work is credited with identifying the correct doses of lithium that are needed for effective treatment.

Blood Clot Filter

A metal alloy called nitinol consisting of nickel and titanium had been created for military and aerospace applications and could be manipulated to change shape at different temperatures. **Morris Simon** began using the alloy in his research in the 1960's to catch and dissolve clots in the bloodstream. In its cold and compact form, Morris' filter is inserted into a patient through a catheter and is expanded to full size when warmed by the patient's body. The filter locks in place near the heart and acts as a sieve to stop blood clots from traveling toward the lungs. The device remains in use today. Among Morris' other innovations was work on a second blood filter that is intended to be removable, a computerized record system for radiology patients, a biopsy needle, a guided catheter and a semi automated system to provide accurate doses of medication to elderly patients.

Streptomycin

Tuberculosis had decimated the world since the time of the pharaohs. It had killed more people than every war, famine and other epidemics all combined. It was considered to be incurable until postgraduate student **Albert Schatz** went into the laboratory in 1943. After only three and a half months he isolated the antibiotic that became known as streptomycin. It was hailed as a miracle drug and considered to be the first effective treatment for tuberculosis. It also was proven to be effective against typhoid and the plague. The laboratory's head biologist took credit for the discovery and Albert had to take him to court to be recognized as a co-discoverer of the drug.

Unlocked Secrets of the Volcano

His work first gained attention while he studied the minerals of Iceland in the 1960's. It greatly advanced the understanding of geology in Iceland and he was awarded the Order of the Falcon by the government in 1977, an honor rarely given to a foreigner. **George Walker**'s greatest achievements came in the study of volcanoes. He arrived at crucial insights into why lava flows in the way it does, why volcanoes are the shape they are and how to begin a study of the hazards posed by volcanoes. Many people considered him to be the father of modern volcanology.

Malaria

It continues to kill up to one million people a year, primarily in Africa. **William Trager** made significant steps toward a better understanding of the disease. As a young researcher he was able to develop a germ-free environment in which to observe mosquitoes. He also found ways to grow insect tissues in order to study sleeping sickness, encephalitis and other diseases carried by insects. In 1976 William cultured the most deadly of the four forms of malaria by using human blood. Hopes were raised that a vaccine could be developed, but a cure still remains elusive. Williams's work was considered a breakthrough that influenced other researchers. He spent 60 years teaching at Rockefeller University.

Botox

In the 1960's **Edward Schantz** worked with highly lethal forms of toxins to identify their usefulness for scientific purposes. His supply of toxin to a research center in San Francisco resulted in approval by the FDA for it to be used as a nonsurgical cure for crossed eyes and clenched eyelids because its application relaxed the eye muscles. The toxin was also found to be effective in dermatology by erasing lines and wrinkles on the faces of patients who wanted cosmetic surgery. The drug is sold commercially as Botox and is also used to treat facial paralysis and spasms.

Early Advocate for AIDS Awareness

In the first part of his career **Alvin Novick** studied the sonar systems of bats. In the second half of the 48 years he spent teaching biology at Yale University he confronted the initial stages of public awareness to AIDS. In the mid-1980's there was a great fear of the disease and discrimination was rampant. In seminars, letters to publications and courses he taught, Alvin reviewed public policies intended to contain the spread of the virus and challenged public officials to face up to the grim reality of the disease. He strongly promoted needle exchanges for intravenous drug users and the protection of the privacy and livelihoods of doctors and other health care workers who became infected as well as also pressing for safeguards in blood banks.

Studied Dying Species

Norman Newell helped to shape the theories surrounding the mass extinction of species. His work began in the 1950's when he reviewed the fossil records of Texas. He also studied the formation and ecology of coral reefs and the geological history of the Peruvian Andes. He proposed that the earth in the late 20th century was experiencing one of the greatest of all mass extinctions. Norman attributed the losses of hundreds of species to ecology disturbances caused by humans. He found a nearly direct correlation between an increase in world population and increasing amounts of carbon dioxide in the atmosphere. In 2004 he was named a Legendary Geoscientist by the American Geological Institute.

The King of Vaccines

Growing up on a farm in Montana, **Maurice Hilleman** credited his success to his boyhood work with chickens whose eggs form the foundation of many vaccines. He developed more human and animal vaccines than anyone and is recognized by many as having saved more lives than any other scientist in the 20th century. He created 8 of the 14 vaccines that are now routinely recommended and developed the first generation of vaccine against German measles. His vaccines have prevented deafness, blindness and other permanent disabilities among millions of people. Maurice was the first to discover how the influenza virus mutated and single handedly developed a vaccine that prevented an Asian flu outbreak in 1957. An outbreak 40 years earlier had killed 20 million people worldwide. President Ronald Reagan presented him with the National Medal of Science in 1988.

Fireflies

Vast displays of fireflies glowing in unison along tidal rivers had been reported for centuries in Southeast Asia and other regions, but had never been recorded or closely studied. **John Buck's** interest in fireflies began in the 1930's when he measured periods between their flashes and studied the effects of temperature and fading daylight on their displays. The glowing of the fireflies is referred to as "bioluminescence" and John traveled throughout Jamaica, Thailand and New Guinea to study their habits. He determined that fireflies were flashing codes of light to one another and synchronized their signals as a mating call for males to attract females. John spent four decades working at the National Institute of Health.

In Vitro Fertilization

She was widely regarded as one of the foremost female scientists in the 20th century. Work that **Georgeanna Jones** performed in the 1930's laid the foundation for the development of home pregnancy tests used by millions of women around the world. Her husband Howard formed a partnership with her that in 1981 produced the first in vitro fertilized baby born in the United States at their clinic in Norfolk, Virginia. More than 114,000 babies have been born through in vitro fertilization in the United States and 3,000 at the Norfolk clinic. She was one of the country's first reproductive endocrinologists and spent four decades at Johns Hopkins School of Medicine where she taught and conducted research.

Researcher of Cancer Gene

Stanley Korsmeyer was one of several scientists in the 1980's to discover a gene that blocks the body's natural process to destroy old or unneeded cells. This process is called programmed cell death and is critical in order to maintain healthy tissue. Stanley studied patients with a common cancer of the immune system and determined that the gene interrupted cell death and let the cancer gene continue to survive. His research allowed a new picture of cancer to emerge. Stanley was elected to the American Academy of Arts and Sciences in 2000 and received the Stratton Medal from the American Society of Hematology in 2004.

Isotopes

Katherine Lathrop was a pioneering researcher in nuclear medicine and a member of a University of Chicago team that developed an isotope that is widely used to locate and diagnose cancers. They experimented with an isotope by injecting it into a patient's bloodstream and then traced it through the brain, heart, kidney and liver. A scan of the isotope revealed images that helped to diagnose and record the size and growth of cancers and other tumors. A scanning system for the isotope was perfected in 1963 and used to perform a successful brain scan. The isotope remains in clinical use worldwide today and is often used to scan bones.

Epilepsy Research

Today it is fairly common knowledge that the brain has two hemispheres, the left controls the right side and vice versa. The right side directs imagination and the left side is considered logical. These concepts grew directly out of the surgeries of **Joseph Bogen.** His work played a crucial role in the development of split-brain experiments that led to a colleague winning the Nobel Prize in 1981 while Joseph's work was overlooked. In severe cases of epilepsy, a structure in the brain known as the corpus callosum can help to overwhelm the brain with seizures. In the early 1960's he and another associate developed a surgery in which the nerve fibers were severed in the corpus callosum and contained the seizure to one hemisphere. The procedure is rarely used, but does control the worst epilepsy symptoms. Joseph was able to show that each side of the brain has independent consciousness and capabilities.

The Mozart Effect

Gordon Shaw was an expert on particle physics before changing his focus to the effects of classical music on higher-level thinking. After twenty years of research Gordon and his collaborators announced in 1993 the results of a study that showed a marked increase in college students' IQ's after they listened to a Mozart sonata. It became known as the Mozart effect, the idea that music can make people smarter. Prenatal music classes and classical CD's for toddlers became the rage. The study, however, showed that the improvement would only last for ten minutes, but Gordon emphasized that Mozart's music was more like a warm-up exercise for parts of the brain that perform high levels of abstract thinking. In 1998 he developed a non-profit institute that developed a curriculum, now in 67 elementary schools, that uses piano keyboard training and a computer program to help the brain become better adjusted to learn math more easily.

Linear Programming

While working for the Air Force in 1947, **George Dantzig** developed the simplex algorithm which enabled decision makers to solve complex problems in an efficient period of time. Although he performed his research using primitive calculators, his work coincided with the development of the computer. George's work was called linear programming and has been used in all sectors of the economy including how to prepare a cost-effective nutritional diet and the coordination of commercial plane routes. He was awarded the National Science Medal in 1975.

Measured Earthquakes

The long-time standard for measuring an earthquake was the Richter scale, but many researchers found that its calculations were not precise. Based on his studies of a 1964 earthquake in Japan. **Keiiti Aki** introduced the seismic moment, a math equation that determines how deep a fault slipped during an earthquake and the length of the slip. The seismic moment is now considered to be the most appropriate way to measure an earthquake's size. Keiiti also was a pioneer in extracting data from seismographs to paint complex pictures of both earthquakes and the Earth. He recorded the data digitally so researchers can now produce three-dimensional maps of the Earth's interior. Keiiti trained more than 60 doctoral and postgraduate students who now hold key scientific positions throughout the world.

Salmonella Researcher

Carlos Hormaeche was a leading international expert in microbiology and vaccine development. Early in his career he began to dissect the precise mechanisms of the natural resistance to a salmonella infection and he worked on unraveling the complex immune response to the infection. Salmonella causes a broad spectrum of diseases from food poisoning to typhoid fever. Carlos was involved in pioneering studies that showed that live salmonella vaccines could be used to take vaccine molecules from diseases other than salmonella and deliver them to the immune system. This helped to produce a multi-use vaccine that could be used to protect against more than one disease at a time. It is still a work in progress with the possibility that a vaccine of this type could enable mass immunizations to be carried out in developing countries against major diseases.

Biologist and Geneticist

Early in his career, **Norman Horowitz** established a reputation for his research on the biochemical evolution of life. Because of that interest, he began a long collaboration, beginning in 1965, with the Jet Propulsion Laboratory in Pasadena, California where he was involved in projects searching for life on other planets. He was best known for creating instruments that were taken to Mars in 1976 for two Viking landings. While serving as a postdoctoral fellow at Stanford University following World War II, Norman worked with two other geneticists in the study of an organism that had not been previously used in genetics research. His two colleagues were awarded the Nobel Prize in 1958 for that work. Norman received a medal from the Genetics Society of America in 1998.

Immunologist

In the early 1950's, **Zoltan Ovary** and his colleagues began a series of experiments that resulted in a strong allergic reaction in the skin of a test animal. The tests enabled them to measure the number of antibodies needed to create an allergic reaction and became a fundamental finding in immunology by allowing science to understand the nature of antibodies that cause the reaction. Zoltan was intrigued by the reaction's benefits and hazards for people and studied the effects of allergic reactions such as hay fever and the benefits that could help people ward off certain parasites. In 1985 he received a distinguished service award from an international allergy association.

The Science of Seeds

Throughout his childhood **John Vaughan** would take long walks and developed a love of plants. He became an expert in seed science which links the fields of botany and nutrition. Spending forty years at the University of London, he pioneered new techniques for the study of seed proteins and became the leading expert on the structures and composition of such crops as cabbage, mustard and oilseed. John's 1970 book on oilseed is still the standard work on the subject.

During the 1970's and '80's when botany was being replaced in interest by more fashionable subjects, John did much to sustain the teaching of plant science, including the use of plant anatomy for identifying ancient seed remains.

Climate Change

Gerard Bond was trained as a classical geologist, but he shifted his interests to the bottom of the ocean floor in the early 1990's when he began to examine samples of sediments retrieved from the North Atlantic. He determined that recent layers had been deposited there by the melting of vast icebergs from eastern Canada. Gerard additionally found that a cycle of warming climates releases glaciers about every 1,500 years and leads to a periodic cooling of the ocean waters by several degrees. He traced this cycle back 100,000 years. Gerard theorized that the 1,500-year cycles were caused by variations in solar activity being driven by solar radiation and sunspots.

The Motion of Stars

The Doppler effect is the shift in frequency and wavelength of light waves and is used to measure the movement of objects in outer space. In the 1970's, **George Isaak** tested Einstein's theory of relativity in an experiment which showed that the velocity of light is constant and independent of the movement of the earth. He devised a method of using the Doppler effect to measure the motion of stars and led to the detection of regular movements within the sun. He discovered that the sun's outer layer weaves in and out with a regular motion and each cycle lasts about five minutes. In doing so, George developed a method of detecting stars and planets within the star's orbit that would otherwise remain invisible. He maintained that if you had enough data about a star, you would know how many planets it had, their size and distance from the star. Ultimately, you would be able to determine which planets were habitable.

Dinosaur Hunter

Until the 1960's dinosaurs were considered to be slow-footed, lazy, cold-blooded and dim-witted reptiles that disappeared from the earth 65 million years ago. **John Ostrom**'s discovery in Montana in 1964 of a dinosaur convinced scientists that they were actually warm-blooded creatures. In 1970 a visit to the Netherlands drew him to the conclusion that birds were descended from dinosaurs. John's work had a profound effect on dinosaur research, shattered stereotypes and inspired sweeping changes in thinking about their lives and times. His work attracted many young researchers to a field that had been moribund for several decades. John's discoveries provided the basis for the book and movie "Jurassic Park".

Plant Genetics

Milton Gordon believed that genetic engineering is the basis for a new agricultural revolution that can be a partial solution for world hunger. As a professor at the University of Washington, he and a colleague were able to prove that a simple bacteria could transform plant cells by introducing a growth hormone gene. With this discovery, other scientists have used his technique to make plants more nutritious and insect resistant. Milton was also one of the first scientists to publish research on the ability of trees and other plants to absorb and neutralize ground based contamination.

Proved How the Stars Shine

Science was aware of the simple set of nuclear reactions that had powered the sun for billions of years, but before **John Bahcall** they had no evidence that the reactions that were taking place in the laboratory were the same as on the sun. In the early 1960's John had performed a series of calculations showing that the sun should be emitting 'neutrinos' that could be detected on Earth. Together with a colleague, they proved what had eluded science for over a century: nuclear reactions that produce neutrinos also cause the sun to shine. John was also instrumental in convincing Congress to spend the money to launch the Hubble Space Telescope in 1990. For years he appeared before Congress to try to convince them of the venture's usefulness. From the time it was first proposed, it took 44 years before the launch took place.

Promethium Ion

Promethium was introduced to the international scientific community after World War II. It is a synthetic and relatively unstable radioactive material and lights up in the dark with a pale blue or green glow. **Jacob Marinsky** and his colleagues isolated it as a form of metal salt. Because it decays rapidly, its discovery was considered astounding so late in the history of science. Due to its glow it was named after the Bringer of Fire, Prometheus. The practical application for this element is in watch dials for their ability to glow in the dark

Ulcer Treatment

Working at the Mayo Clinic, **Horace Davenport** in the 1960's explored the stomach's lining to determine why the acid that is produced during digestion doesn't destroy the stomach in the process. The experiments led to a break-through in understanding the mechanics of digestion. Horace found that aspirin and other substances caused hydrogen to flood into the cells of the stomach's pro-tective barrier and caused salt to leave the cells and result in an ulcer. A decade later, drug companies used his findings to create a new generation of stomach medications to protect the stomach barrier and prevent peptic ulcers.

Pushed the Potato

She wanted to dispel the notion that it was a weighty clump of empty calories. **Nell Mondy** was drawn to the potato by its nutritional richness, low cost and long shelf life. In 40 years at Cornell University, Nell compared the taste of dif-ferent varieties of potatoes and promoted their value as a staple food that could provide protein, calcium, vitamin C, iron and other nutrients. In the 1990's she also reported on the health hazards of potato skins when she found that chemicals sprayed on potatoes to prevent sprouting in storage often got to the grocery store in significantly higher levels that recommended federal guidelines. Nell promoted potatoes as a crop for developing countries, particularly in Africa.

Child Obesity

Until **Ruth Huenemann** began her research, the popular belief was that over-weight babies became obese adults. Her study of 1,000 students over a four-year period found that the amount of exercise was the determining factor in adult obe-sity. Nearly ten years later a second study was conducted that found children were exercising less than ever due to their fascination with television and cars. Ruth got detailed information on what they ate, their physical exercise, body composition and relationship with their parents. All of these were details that had not been tracked in the past. She was among the first to identify what is now a national crisis.

Glaucoma Detection

The disease is a major cause of blindness throughout the world. Glaucoma devel-ops by unregulated pressure within the eye on the optic nerve which cuts blood circulation and causes permanent damage to the nerve to the point of blindness. While a graduate student in the 1950's, **Mansour Armaly** noticed the poor state of glaucoma research and began a study of people who did not have the disease. It would last 13 years, but after only two years the initial results were so startling that a national study was begun, which he led. The research focused on damage to the optic nerve, the role of genetics in eye disease and other factors that contributed to glaucoma. Mansour's work developed a standard method of measuring the field of vision and the early detection of glaucoma.

Weather Forecasting

Before the development of computers in the 1950's, weather could only be predicted for the next day or two. A long time theory held that weather data plugged into a computer would greatly improve forecasting. By combining math models with a computer, **Joseph Smagorinksy** was able to extend weather prediction and identify trends in the global climate. His models included wind, cloud cover, rain, atmospheric pressure and radiation coming from the earth and sun. In the 1970's Joseph and his colleagues predicted a historic trend in warming that was borne out decades later with the rapid melting of the Arctic ice masses. In 2003 he was awarded the Benjamin Franklin Medal in Earth Science.

Brain Disorders

In late 1950's in England, interest was heightened on what effect interference of the blood supply to the brain would have during heart surgery. It was well established that a good supply of blood was needed, but it was difficult to determine how much was actually moving through. **Murray Harper**'s work led to a better understanding of how the process worked and how it changes in the case of disease. His findings led to advances in the care of patients with brain disorders. Based on his concepts, measurements of the brain's blood flow during operations were used to predict a patient's risk of stroke.

SOCIAL INFLUENCE

The Deconstructionist

His message: language is inadequate to give a clear view of reality. **Jacques Derrida** believed that a collection of words is not fixed and unchanging, but could have many interpretations. He was best known for his comment, "there is nothing outside the text". Jacques was a French philosopher whose influence spanned across the globe. His theory of deconstruction held that writing had so much contradiction and confusion that the author could never overcome the inherent conflicts of language and was unable to provide an obvious meaning. His concept was applied to other fields, such as architecture.

First Black US Admiral

He was a trailblazer throughout his career which began as a fireman apprentice in the Naval Reserve in 1942. After the end of World War II, **Samuel Gravely** finished his college education and resumed active duty at the end of the decade to help recruit African-Americans for the newly desegregated Navy. During the course of his 38 years with the Navy, Samuel became the first black man to command a Navy warship when he became skipper of the destroyer Falgout. In 1962 he and another officer were the first two African-Americans to attend the prestigious Naval War College. In 1976 he became a vice admiral when he was assigned command of the Navy's Third Fleet in the Pacific overseeing 100 ships and 60,000 sailors. Samuel received the Legion of Merit, Bronze Star, Meritorious Service Medal and the Navy Commendation Medal.

Drug Treatment Program

Alexander Bassin was a social worker and criminologist working in the probation Department of the State Supreme Court in Brooklyn in 1963. He was concerned with the inability of the prison system to rehabilitate drug addicts. Taking matters into his own hands, Alexander, and the court's chief probation officer, founded Daytop Lodge. It was created as a halfway house for drug addicts in a 20-room mansion on Staten Island. It is now the oldest continuing residential drug treatment program in the United States and has accepted over 100,000 people. It became known as Daytop Village in 1964 and admitted men and women in addition to non-probationers.

Encouraged Understanding between Cultures

She was born and raised a Muslim in Philadelphia. **Sharifa Alkhateeb** explained the ways of Islam to the United States and the world. She worked as a scholar, journalist and educator and embraced both the American and Islamic cultures in an effort to bring them closer together. Sharifa advised schools, police departments, corporations, government agencies and book publishers on the nature of Islamic life. She co-wrote the Arab World Notebook which is used widely in the public school system in the US. She founded the Peaceful Families Project that is sponsored by the US Department of Justice to study violence in the Muslim community. Sharifa was also president of the Muslim Education Council that advised public school teachers on Islamic life and also persuaded several high schools in Virginia to include Arabic as a language course offering to students.

Gave Support to Cancer Patients

A mother of two, **Shannon McGowan** first got cancer at 35. She was disappointed by the scarce amount of resources available to survivors in the early 1980's. Trained as a school teacher, after recovering she earned a masters degree in psychotherapy and, with a partner, opened a Wellness Community in Santa Monica, California to offer emotional support. The initial center grew into a network of 21 centers across the United States as well as programs in Tokyo and Tel Aviv. The centers offer support groups, education and relaxation workshops to help cancer patients take an active role in working with their doctor toward recovery.

Used Sports to Educate

In the late 1960's, **Tulley Brown** left a career in business to work with emotionally disturbed children. He began raising money and building a library collection for a halfway house for youths facing legal problems. During this time he developed the idea for Direction Sports. The program was geared toward disadvantaged youths and used their interest in sports to challenge them in math and other academic subjects. It began as an after school activity for elementary and junior high school students where teams studied before practice on school days and competed on the weekends in academics. College students provided the tutoring and coaching with many doing it on a volunteer basis. Students would be asked to spell such sports oriented words as 'field goal' or 'rebound' and solve math problems by using sports examples. A yearlong study conducted by a UCLA professor found that students in the program showed a marked improvement in test scores over students who did not participate. Direction Sports was expanded into other cities including New York, Chicago and Atlanta.

The Storyteller

The situation was near desperation. Filling in for the regular story lady, **Jackie Torrence** couldn't come up with a story to the liking of a small group of five-year-olds. She pulled a story out of her past from the cultural lore of her Appalachian childhood and the kids were hooked. She quickly became the full-time story lady and later catapulted onto the national stage as word grew of her talents. She would travel three-quarters of each year around the USA appearing in every state. Jackie once got her own nationally televised special and appeared on network news and interview shows. Fortune 500 companies used her services to teach their sales teams how to communicate in simple terms.

Little Colonel

She had to stand on the tips of her toes to meet the height requirement. **Mary Hallaren** left 15 years of teaching behind when Pearl Harbor was attacked and joined the military. Mary commanded the first battalion of the Women's Army Corps in Europe during World War II. It was also the largest unit of women to serve overseas. She was among a group of officer who convinced Congress in 1948 to integrate women into the regular armed services. She was the first woman to be sworn in as an officer and served until 1960. In retirement, Mary helped to organize Women in Community Service which became a national non-profit to help women and children in poverty or living on the edge of society. She was inducted into the Women's Hall of Fame in 1996.

Theoretical Scientist

His theories could be controversial, but he was well respected for his contributions to science. **H. Bentley Glass** wrote more than 400 scientific articles in his career and wrote a science column for the Baltimore Sun. He was regarded as one of the top geneticists during his 18 years at Johns Hopkins University and 11 years at SUNY-Stony Brook. For 3 years he also was the national president of Phi Beta Kappa. His theory of genetic drift stated that it was not necessary to classify anyone by race. He predicted test tube babies nearly twenty years before the first test tube birth. He argued for controls on population growth and pointed out the harmful effects of radiation from nuclear bomb tests.

United Cerebral Palsy

Her daughter was born with cerebral palsy. In 1945 **Isabelle Goldenson** and her husband placed an ad in The New York Herald Tribune looking for other parents whose children had the disease. Along with another couple, they founded United Cerebral Palsy four years later. Isabelle also co-founded the organization's Research and Educational Foundation which contributed to the discovery of the vaccine against German measles and development of the fetal heart monitor. Soon after NASA put a man on the moon in 1969, Isabelle met with their scientists and engineers to create a lightweight wheelchair, remote control limbs and sensory devices to help blind people. Nearly twenty years before the Americans With Disabilities Act was passed in 1990, she lobbied for an amendment to a law that for the first time prohibited discrimination on the basis of disability. Today, United Cerebral Palsy provides daily services to more than 30,000 people.

Arms Control Activist

Working at the University of Chicago in the early 1950's, **Ruth Adams** became acquainted with scientists who had played a role in the creation of the atomic age. With no background in physics, she attended the first Pugwash conference which brought together eminent scientists from 10 countries that were concerned about the nuclear threat. Although she had a tough learning curve, Ruth eventually became editor of the Bulletin of the Atomic Scientists on two occasions. The publication voiced the need to take seriously the dangers of nuclear weapons. Her ambition and contacts played a role in the launching of an International Centre in Kenya which has trained more than 160 African scientists over a 30-year period on issues related to pest management.

Founded Center for Alcoholics

Lesbians are believed to have a higher rate of alcoholism than the general population. Decades ago they were turned away from traditional recovery programs which were dominated by men. **Brenda Weathers** was expelled from Texas Women's University in 1957 after officials there found out that she was a lesbian. She moved to California, but turned to drinking to deal with the burden of keeping her sexuality a secret. Brenda became a recovered alcoholic and founded the

Alcoholism Center for Women in 1974, the first facility in the United States to serve primarily gay women. Three years later she moved to San Francisco to run a similar operation and later was the director of the Gay and Lesbian Chemical Dependency Program in Seattle.

Hostage Negotiation Unit

The old method was to kick in the door or threaten to throw in tear gas. As a result, people and police were killed. As commanding officer of the New York City police department's special operations division, **Simon Eisdorfer** conceived the idea of a negotiating team after watching the tragedy unfold during the 1972 Olympic Games when 12 Israeli athletes were taken hostage and killed. Simon realized that New York City had the same vulnerability and introduced the team in 1973 following a high profile standoff a few months earlier in which protracted negotiation had minimized the conflict. Simon's approach emphasized saving lives by turning a siege into a waiting game where the suspect would eventually tire out and surrender. Police officials across the US visited the NYPD for training. The methods put in place by Simon are still in use today.

Amnesty International

On a November evening in 1960 **Peter Benenson** got on the London Underground train and read the story of two students in Portugal who were sentenced to seven years in jail for having made a toast to liberty in the then-dictator led country. Several months later he wrote an article in the London Observer encouraging people to spend the next year on a letter writing campaign to encourage the release of "prisoners of conscience" throughout the world. Thousands joined the call and the effort expanded rapidly. In the first five years, Peter ran the organization, provided most of the money and traveled extensively to investigate cases and promote Amnesty's cause to the media. He stepped down from active involvement in 1966. Today the organization has 1.8 million members in 64 countries. Amnesty International was awarded the Nobel Peace Prize in 1977.

The SNCC

Many times he was harassed, jailed and beaten when he tried to register black voters in the Deep South in the 1960's. At the height of the civil rights movement, **James Forman** created a role for the Student Nonviolent Coordinating Committee among the so-called Big Five established civil rights organizations. During his association with the SNCC from 1961 to 1966, James was responsible for making sure that organizers were fed, housed and transported from one southern town to the next, getting them out of jail when needed and raising money for the SNCC's continued existence. In later years he founded a nonprofit company called the Unemployment and Poverty Action Committee.

Helped Airline Hostages

There is no greater example of courage than **Uli Derickson**. On June 14, 1985 Lebanese gunmen hijacked a plane from Athens to Rome. Uli was a flight attendant for T.W.A airlines. For 36 hours she both confronted and calmed the hijackers and saved many lives in the process. The hijackers spoke no English, but Uli was able to converse with one in German and would calm him by singing a German ballad he had requested. During a refueling stop in Algiers the ground crew refused to put gas in the plane without being paid and the terrorists threatened to begin killing people. Uli gave them her Shell credit card and they charged it $5,500 for 6,000 gallons of fuel. She was released in the second wave of hostages in Algiers. Despite the experience she continued to work as a flight attendant. Uli was the first woman to receive the Silver Cross of Valor, awarded by the Legion of Valor, a veteran's organization.

Korean Anthem

Mary Kim Joh attended American missionary schools in Korea. Following the end of the Japanese occupation in World War II, the country had no Korean language school materials. She was the director of the music department at Ewha Women's University at the time and was asked by the South Korean government to compose children's songs. "School Bells" was written in 1945 and became an anthem that, to this day, is required to be learned by all students attending grammar school in South Korea. Mary moved to New York in 1978 and began a program called "Spoons for Liberia" which sent sanitary utensils to the country in an effort to curb tropical diseases there. At age 73, she joined the Peace Corps and worked in a Liberian hospital 600 miles from the country's capital city of Monrovia.

Teen Help Line

Terry Lipton knew that a teen in trouble would turn first to another teen for advice. As chairman of a program affiliated with Cedars-Sinai Medical Center in Los Angeles, he co-founded "Teen Line" in 1981, a confidential phone help line staffed by trained teenage volunteers who are supervised by mental health professionals. Since its founding nearly 400,000 calls have been placed to Teen Line which also offers a program for teen volunteers to give presentations to schools and youth groups that serve adolescents. Terry himself overcame hurdles in his personal life when he contracted polio at the age of 4. The same year Teen Line was founded he climbed on crutches to the base camp of Mount Everest at 18,000 feet. He later climbed Mt. Etna in Sicily, climbed pyramids in Mexico and pulled himself up by rope to visit Buddhist caves above the Mekong River in Laos.

Community Gardens

He grew up on a 15-acre farm in Germany. After working as a psychoanalyst, landscape architect and university professor, **Karl Linn** came to believe that architecture should reflect a deep commitment to social justice. In 1961 he founded the Neighborhood Renewal Corps which assisted disadvantaged communities in reclaiming, designing and rebuilding blighted urban spaces. Begun in Philadelphia, the gardens grew to other cities around the United States. His gardens were noted for their use of native plants, bubbling fountains, colorful mosaics and benches positioned to encourage face-to-face contact.

The Woolworth's Sit-In

Memphis Norman was a student at a small college in Mississippi in 1963 when he was encouraged by the NAACP to join in a civil rights protest at a Woolworth's lunch counter in Jackson, Mississippi. He joined four others to protest segregated facilities in the South. A local radio station called for bigots to come and harass the demonstrators. For three hours Memphis and his associates were dragged off their lunch stools, but they kept going back to sit. At first they were doused with mustard, salt, sugar and spray paint, but the bigots actions turned extremely violent and they began to beat them with fists, brass knuckles and jagged pieces of broken sugar containers. They also burned them with cigarettes. A former policeman knocked Memphis off his seat and kicked him in the face, chest and abdomen. A photo of the altercation was published in newspapers around the country. For the rest of his life Memphis suffered a lifelong throbbing in his head. He would tell people that day was much worse than anything he experienced during his later tour of duty in Vietnam. The lunch counter protest was one of the defining moments of the civil rights struggle and prompted Martin Luther King, Jr. to begin considering a mass march on Washington, DC which did take place two years later.

Asian American Activist

In the late 1930's as a personnel examiner with the Los Angeles Civil Service Commission, **K. Patrick Okura** occupied the highest city office held by a Japanese American. With the onset of World War II he and his wife were forced into a relocation center along with 120,000 other Japanese Americans living on the West Coast. They would remain in the center for 9 months until he was recruited by Father Flanagan's Boys Town in Nebraska to work as a psychologist. He stayed in the state until 1970 when he joined the National Institute of Mental Health in Washington, DC. Over the next 15 years K. Patrick tackled a wide range of projects, including an assessment of the mental health needs of Vietnamese refugees in resettlement programs after the fall of Saigon. He also helped to create ethnic task forces and scholarships for minorities who wanted to become mental health professionals. He played a major role in an initiative to establish community-based training programs for Asian American social workers and later helped launch the Asian American Psychological Association. His crowning achievement was the creation of the Okura Mental Health Leadership Foundation which gathers a group of Asian American mental health professionals once a year to meet top policymakers in Washington and develop leadership skills.

Gay Rights Pioneer

In the early 1960's a gay man or a lesbian risked being jailed or institutionalized and identifying yourself in public as being gay posed serious risks. **Jack Nichols** co-founded the Washington Mattachine Society in 1961, an early gay advocacy group that helped to create the mindset for public expression of dissent by gay people. In 1965 Jack and nine others held a protest in front of the White House against government discrimination in hiring gays. It was considered to be the first gay rights march. A few years later he became one of the first Americans to talk openly about his homosexuality when he appeared in a CBS documentary. Jack also successfully lobbied the American Psychiatric Association to rescind its definition of homosexuality as a form of mental illness.

The Responsibility of Scientists

In the mid-1960's **John Ziman** became a leading advocate of the view that scientists needed to communicate better with the public, avoid jargon and write so that the general public could understand them. Nearly twenty years later he spearheaded a campaign to stir scientists to take a public stand over the treatment of their colleagues in the then-Soviet Union who had been fired from their jobs and prohibited from traveling due to political reasons. During the same time period John was recognized for his work in identifying the abuse of the human rights of scientists in the signatory countries to the Helsinki agreement.

Defeated Segregation

He was the first black to earn a doctorate in psychology from Columbia University, the first to become a tenured instructor in the City College system of New York and the first black elected to the New York Sate Board of Regents. As early as 1939 **Kenneth Clark** and his wife had begun conducting tests to assess black youngsters' self-perception. He found that they saw themselves as inferior and they accepted their inferiority as part of reality. Eleven years later a new study still found the same result. In the landmark 1954 Supreme Court decision, Brown v. Board of Education, which struck down segregation, the court used Kenneth's findings in its ruling that "separate but equal" was unconstitutional. Through the years mayors and governors consulted Kenneth and he expressed his views about every racial matter from school busing to housing discrimination.

Innovator in Opinion Polling

The pollsters all agreed, Republican candidate Thomas Dewey would defeat President Harry Truman in the 1948 presidential election. The only problem was that they were all wrong with Truman winning in a so-called upset. Out of the wreckage of the polling industry came two landmark innovations from **Paul Perry** that restored credibility. The need to devise a system to identify likely voters and being able to determine a method to allocate undecided voters to candidates were the cornerstones of Paul's recommendations. He worked in association with the Gallup poll organization for 45 years. Paul also pioneered a method to project a movie's eventual gross revenue based on the public's awareness, interest, marquee value and audience enjoyment through test audiences. He is also credited with the creation of the Likely Voters Index, a seven-question survey that is still considered the most valid method to predict whether a person will actually vote in an election.

First Black Marine Officer

Frederick Branch was drafted in 1942 while a student at Temple University in Philadelphia. He scored well on a test for Officer Candidate School, but was rejected because he did not have a recommendation. His wartime service in the Pacific did get him the recommendation he needed and Frederick was commissioned as a Marine lieutenant on November 10, 1945, the 170th anniversary of the founding of the corps in Philadelphia. He was the only black graduate in a class of 250 and became the first black commissioned officer in the Marine Corps.

Lawyer to the Indigent

One night while camping during a trip to Afghanistan, **Thomas Concannon** watched herdsmen lead a caravan of camels across the sand. To him, he was reminded of the shallowness of materialism. Returning to America, he spent the next three decades as an attorney with the Legal Aid Society defending thousands of poor people in New York. He oversaw an office that annually represents 1,000 indigent people and personally handled up to 80 cases a year himself. Since 1980 it was estimated that Thomas had a hand in defending more than 20,000 people who could not afford a lawyer.

Fought to Keep Ancestral Lands

A treaty signed in 1863 by the Indian Shoshone chiefs and ratified by the United States Senate allowed white settlers to cross Indian lands to establish a way of life there. But the treaty did not transfer ownership of the land to the US government. Moving far ahead to 1962, the Indian Claims Commission, established by Congress, concluded that Shoshone land had been lost due to the gradual encroachment of white settlers. **Mary Dann** refused to accept that ruling and fought for three decades, along with her sister, against the Bureau of Land Management. She tried to reclaim 24 million acres that she considered ancestral land that stretched from Idaho into California. The battle was ongoing and, despite court decisions, had not been resolved. In 1993 she received the international Right Livelihood Award from a Stockholm based organization in recognition of her courage in fighting for the rights of indigenous people.

Led Civil Rights at the YWCA

When **Helen Claytor** first went to work for the YWCA in the 1930's, she had to join the separate "Negro" branch of the segregated facility in Kansas City, Missouri. She later moved to New York City as a member of their newly established office of race relations and campaigned throughout the South to try and desegregate the local Y's. By 1949 Helen was elected president of the Grand Rapids YWCA and three board members resigned in protest. In 1967 she was elected national president of the organization, becoming the first African—American woman as its head. Helen was inducted into the Michigan Women's Hall of Fame.

Advocate for Self-Sufficient Women

She spent her professional life directing organizations that fought for equal pay, financial self-sufficiency and access to nontraditional jobs for women. **Cindy Marano** developed legislative proposals and testified before Congress on job training, welfare-to-work and vocational education. She helped to create women's literacy programs and guided Wider Opportunities for Women to pursue jobs in the construction trade and other jobs not normally filled by women. Her efforts contributed to four federal laws. Cindy developed the Self-Sufficiency Standard which some states use to decide living wages based on the number and age of children and geographic areas.

The Effect of Adoption on Birth Mothers

Sue Whitworth-Jackson twice had to give up children to adoption to whom she had given birth. She would later raise two children of her own, but never got over the pain of giving up her first two children. She would later reunite with them in adulthood, but wanted to use her personal experience to help other women cope. Working with the National Parents Network, Sue partnered with other organizations to help mothers who wanted to contact their children. Many women had been pressured or forced to give up their children in England from the 1950's to the 1970's and had been treated with disrespect. Sue lobbied Parliament and helped to trigger the most radical overhaul of adoption laws in a quarter century. In 2002, the Adoption and Children Act, for the first time, gave birth relatives the right to an intermediary service to inform an adult adopted person that they are interested in making contact.

Statewide Opinion Surveys

Opinion surveys were once looked upon as simply making an educated guess. As a student in the 1930's, with an interest in scientific sampling, **Joe Belden** corresponded with the now legendary pollster George Gallup and other early practitioners to learn how to hone his craft. Using their advice, he started the Texas Poll to gauge public opinion about social issues of the day as well as politics and elections. He sold his findings to newspapers across the state and the Texas Poll became a model for other regional and state surveys. In Mexico in 1947 he used opinion surveys to devise the country's first radio and television rating system. In the early '90's Joe received the lifetime achievement award of the American Association for Public Opinion Research.

Rights Activist

After five years of life in a convent, **Jean O'Leary** decided that she was more suited to the life of a layperson and left the convent to move to Greenwich Village in New York City. She became heavily involved in a number of prominent gay and lesbian organizations. By 1976 she had become the first openly gay lesbian delegate at a Democratic National Convention. With the election of Jimmy Carter as president, Jean used her contacts in the administration to arrange a meeting with Carter in 1977 to discuss gay issues in healthcare and the military and also cover discriminatory laws. It was the first time a president had agreed to meet a group of gay activists.

The Smokeout

Don't Smoke Days were founded by **Lynn Smith** when he was the publisher of the Monticello Times in Minnesota in the 1970's. He called it 'D-Day' (Don't Smoke Day) and it was first held on January 6, 1974. When three hundred people pledged to stop smoking or using tobacco Lynn put their names on the front page of his newspaper. Three months later 90% said they had quit smoking. That same year the Minnesota Lung Association and the American Cancer Society worked with Lynn to begin a statewide campaign. Within two years the cancer society took it nationwide and The Great American Smokeout is now held each year on the third Thursday of November.

Hospice Care

It was in a London hospital in the late 1940's that **Cicely Saunders** became friendly with a survivor of the Warsaw ghetto in World War II who was slowly dying. They talked about the lack of care given to patients who neared the end of life. Little was known then about the management of pain and hospices provided comfort, but did little to alleviate the suffering. He left her the little money he had. Cicely graduated from medical school at age 39 and in 1967 opened St. Christopher's Hospice. It pioneered research on the use of morphine for pain control, became the first teaching hospice and Cicely was a recognized authority on care for the dying. In 1997 she became the first person in more than 100 years to receive an honorary doctorate of medicine from the Archbishop of Canterbury. In 1980 she had been named a dame of the British Empire by Queen Elizabeth and received the Templeton Prize the following year, considered the equivalent of the Nobel Prize for religion.

Black Stuntmen

During the filming of the movie "It's a Mad Mad Mad Mad World" in 1963, **Edward Smith** saw a white stuntman in makeup being made up to become a stunt double for a black actor. He organized a group of black re-enactors of the Buffalo Soldiers and trained them in the art of stunt work and, in 1967, the Black Stuntmen's Association was formed. Following a confrontation with Warner Brothers in 1971, the studio agreed to hire black stunt people to double for black actors and include black stuntmen in all scenes involving general stunt work. They also invited black stuntmen to train with veteran white stuntmen. During his career, Edward worked as a stuntman or stunt coordinator on many TV shows and movies including, "MASH, "Dirty Harry", "Blazing Saddles, "Scarface" and "Roots".

Helped Abused Children

For over fifty years, **Vincent Fontana** helped to define the problems and scope of child neglect in the United States. An author of many books and articles on the subject, he became the medical director and principal pediatrician in 1959 of what became known as the New York Foundling, a social service agency serving thousands of people from newborns to adults. In 1998 he started the Vincent J. Fontana Center for Child Protection to further understand and detect child abuse and neglect and to teach its prevention and treatment. He was involved in numerous programs of foster care and adoption services and prenatal care for expectant mothers. His innovative approach set a pattern for other institutions.

Affirmative Action

In 1950's Kansas, **Arthur Fletcher** saw firsthand that better access to lucrative government contracts was the cornerstone to improving the prospects of minorities. Making his way through the political world, he became an Assistant Secretary of Labor in 1969 and implemented what became known as the Philadelphia Plan, a program to enforce the hiring of minorities by businesses and trade unions contracted by the government. By requiring the government to set timetables and goals in the hiring of minority workers, Arthur set in motion the framework for affirmative action. He also served as executive director of the United Negro College Fund. While there it was said that he helped to coin the fundraising slogan, "a mind is a terrible thing to waste". A staunch defender of education, Arthur personally helped to finance the lawsuit against the Topeka Board of Education in the landmark Brown v. Board of Education case in 1954 which struck down the 'separate but equal' doctrine and began the process of desegregation in American society.

Public Health Advocate

Ruth Roemer recognized before many people the untapped potential for changes in laws and regulations to improve and protect public health. Starting in the 1960's she turned her focus to health law after participating in a landmark study of the laws governing admission to mental hospitals in New York state. Moving to California she helped to spearhead a law that legalized abortion under special cases. Ruth also became prominent in campaigns to add fluoride to public water supplies in the US and pushed the World Health Organization to focus on controlling the use of tobacco.

Broke Barriers at the Opera

It was an unintentional accident that introduced **Helen Phillips** as the first black singer to appear with the Metropolitan Opera Chorus in New York City in 1947. Her agent had been contacted by the stage manager to send a replacement soprano. When Helen arrived she was given a quick glance and told to go backstage to get ready. She preceded Marian Anderson in breaking color barriers at different venues in the 1940's and 50's. Helen also became the first African-American soloist with the Edwin Goldman band that played in Central Park during that time. After World War II she made more than 500 concert appearances for the State Department in Austria and West Germany.

Toys for Tots

In 1947 **Jon Riffel**, a public relations executive for a southern California gas company, teamed up with his publicist friend at Warner Brothers studios to form a toy drive to benefit underprivileged children. With the involvement of Marine Corps reservists in the Los Angeles area, five thousand toys were collected that first year. By 2004, 19 million toys were collected at Christmas time and distributed to 7.5 million children.

Moral Opposition to Nuclear Weapons

He felt he had no choice. Permanently leaving his native Poland the day before Germany invaded in 1939 to start World War II, **Joseph Rotblat** would become a member of the British team that worked on the Manhattan Project which built the first atomic bombs. He justified his work because he felt that Hitler needed to be stopped. After nine months he left the project in opposition to the ramifications of their work. Joseph would devote the rest of his life to a worldwide campaign to eliminate nuclear weapons, culminating in being awarded the Nobel Peace Prize in 1995. In 1957 Joseph and other scientists held the Pugwash Conferences which, through the decades, would press to diminish the part played by nuclear arms in international politics and to eventually eliminate nuclear weapons.

A Life of Landmarks

She was the first black woman to argue a case before the Supreme Court, serve in the New York State Senate and become Manhattan borough president. **Constance Baker Motley** also fought nearly every important civil rights case in a twenty-year period at the height of the movement to include blacks in social participation. She visited Martin Luther King Jr. while he was in jail, sang freedom songs in churches that had been bombed and spent a night under armed guard with Medger Evers, a civil rights leader who would later on be murdered. Constance won cases that ended segregation in Memphis restaurants and at whites-only lunch counters in Birmingham, AL. She directed the legal campaign that led to the admission of James Meredith at the University of Mississippi in 1962. Of the ten cases she argued before the Supreme Court, she won nine.

SPORTS

The First Latin Batting Champion

As a youth he had dreamed of being a bullfighter, but followed a more stable path by studying engineering at the University of Mexico. His athletic ability took him to the United States and a career as a major league baseball player. **Bobby Avila** became the first Mexican and Latin to win a batting title when he led the American League in hitting in 1954. He became the role model for other Latinos who followed his path to play baseball in the United States. He was a three-time all-star and played in the major leagues for 11 years before returning to Mexico and pursuing a second career as a member of the Mexican legislature and mayor of Veracruz.

Blind Skier

By the age of 5 she had lost the sight in both of her eyes. Undeterred, **Cara Dunne-Yates** learned to ride the bicycle the same year she became completely blind. She went on to graduate from Harvard University and was elected class president. A law degree from UCLA was next. Cara also learned to ski while she was young and won 13 Paralympic and world championship medals. She was honored as a True Hero of Sport in 2002 by Northeastern University's Center for the Study of Sports.

Jogging

Arthur Lydiard dropped out of school to make women's shoes. He ran cross-country as a boy and would use distance running to get in shape for his favorite sport, rugby. He began to win marathons in his home country of New Zealand as a result of his training routine that became known as L.S.D.—long, slow, distance. It called for running up to 100 miles a week with hill running and speed work as the race drew nearer. At the time the practice was considered controversial. Arthur maintained that a high level of aerobic activity at a constant pace aided the body's ability to use oxygen and would help a runner compete in middle distance events to marathons. He spread his methods by traveling widely in the 1960's and early 1970's and preached the advantages of jogging. He stressed that the method was just as effective for the average person who was only interested in staying in shape.

The Pitching Machine

He is an honorary member of the baseball Hall of Fame and held eight baseball product patents. In 1952 **Larry Ponza** developed the "Power Pitcher" which was the first modern pitching machine. His other inventions included "The Port-O-Pitch" in 1960, the "Casey" in 1983, the "Ponza Swing King" in '87 and the "Rookie" in '88. Larry was best known for his 1974 "Hummer" that became the benchmark batting-practice tool. A baseball placed into two spinning plates formed in a "V" position could mimic a fastball, ground ball and pop fly. It became the standard pitching machine from Little League up through Major League baseball.

The Globetrotters

Basketball began at the age of six. By 1942 he became only the third white member of the Harlem Globetrotters and the first white player under contract. **Bob Karstens** created several of their signature routines including the pregame 'Magic Circle' as well as the backhand shot, the 'yo-yo' basketball and the 'goofball', a basketball filled with weights that makes it bounce erratically. He played for a year and a half until a Globetrotter regular returned from the service and stayed on as team manager another 11 years. In 1994 Bob was awarded the organization's "Legends" ring.

Breeders' Cup

Raising horses had been a way of life for his family back to his grandfather. Following graduation from Notre Dame and a post-graduate degree in genetics at the University of Kentucky, **John Gaines** joined the family enterprise. He was best known as the inventor of the Breeders' Cup in the early 1980's, eight races with multi-million dollar purses that are considered the world's championship in horse racing. In the 1990's he became the founding director of an organization which developed into the National Thoroughbred Racing Association which oversees the marketing for US based thoroughbred racing. John was elected into the Kentucky Athletic Hall of Fame in 1992.

Father of Dutch Football

At age 18 he began playing for the Holland soccer team Ajax. By 1965 **Rinus Michels** had become the team's coach and led them to 4 Dutch championships, 3 Dutch Cups and the European cup. As coach of the national team, the Netherlands won the European Championship in 1988. He introduced a system where players could change roles and improvise and were not locked into one position. He carried this style over to the national team which earned their play the term "clockwork orange". In 1999 Rinus was named coach of the century by world soccer's governing body, FIFA.

Integrated Oklahoma Football

They were in the middle of the longest winning streak in college football history and had no black players on the team. The University of Oklahoma had begun admitting black students on a nonsegregated basis in 1950 and had dropped all restrictions by 1955. One year later **Prentice Gautt** joined the team as a non-scholarship player, attending the college with money contributed by a group of black doctors and pharmacists as head coach Bud Wilkinson had been pressured against giving Prentice a scholarship. As a high school student he had played in the first integrated game in the state and was the first black player in the state all-star game. By 1958 he was considered the best player on the team and was the Most Valuable Player in the 1959 Orange Bowl as well as being named to the academic All-American team. He would go on to earn masters and doctorate degrees. In 1987 the University awarded him the Distinguished Service Citation, their highest honor, for conducting himself with dignity and integrity. By 1999 the Dr. Prentice Gautt Academic Center was dedicated and four years later he received an honorary doctorate for his years of service to college athletics and student athletes.

Mr. Outside

Many people called him the best athlete they ever saw. **Glenn Davis** won 10 varsity letters in four sports at West Point during World War II, but his recognition came in playing college football with some of the best teams to ever play the sport. He was called "Mr. Outside" for his speed and won the Heisman Trophy in 1946 (he was twice the runner-up), the same year he became the first college football player to be named the male athlete of the year by the Associated Press. He also posted the highest score that had ever been attained on the academy's physical proficiency test. Sixty years later he still holds the college football career record for the highest number of yards gained for each rushing attempt. Glenn's greatest contribution came in making the millions of Army soldiers fighting the war feel a little bit better as they heard and read of the legendary exploits of his accomplishments as he represented the Army on the playing field.

Conquered the Swiss Alps

The north face of the Eiger mountaintop in the Swiss Alps was called the "death wall" by the press. The government of Switzerland passed a law forbidding an attempt to climb it, but protestors forced its repeal. The 6,000-foot wall posed a combination of crumbling rock, ice and loose snow that required techniques that were ahead of their time. Above the wall was the 13,000-foot summit. By 1938 only three people had survived of the twelve people who had attempted to climb it. **Anderl Heckmair** was a German mountain guide who led a team on the first successful ascent of the North Face of the Eiger in July 1938. He led the climb in the most difficult sections and navigated their way through the labyrinth of ice gullies. His achievement is considered to be one of the finest moments in alpine mountaineering.

Cowgirl

Bobby Brooks Kramer and her husband ranched for a living in Montana and would ship up to 10,000 horses a year. Known throughout Montana and the West as an excellent horsewoman and savvy rancher, she was one of the first women to ride broncos for prize money. In the 1950's she finished a one-day, one-rider, one-horse endurance race from Billings to Miles City, a distance of 145 miles. Nearly 40 years later she rode with the drivers moving cattle from Roundup to Billings on the Great Montana Centennial Cattle Drive. In 2000 she was inducted into The National Cowgirl Museum and Hall of Fame in Forth Worth.

Legendary Bowler

He only weighed 130 pounds and was 5 feet 10 inches. **Dick Weber** became one of bowling's biggest stars in the 1960's when it became a major attraction on Saturday afternoon television. In 1959 he had become a charter member of the Professional Bowlers Association. He would go on to win 26 PBA tournaments and six titles on the Senior Tour. He was voted bowler of the year three times in the early 1960's. To promote the sport Dick bowled on the beach in Miami Beach and on a cargo plane. He appeared on David Letterman and rolled bowling balls into ketchup, beer bottles and lava lamps. He also traveled the world on behalf of the sport. In 1999, Bowling Magazine voted Dick the best bowler of the 20th century. He was inducted into two bowling Halls of Fame in the 1970's.

Batting Helmets

Charlie Muse worked for the Pittsburgh Pirates for 52 years. One of his assignments during his tenure was to run the American Baseball Cap company that was owned by legendary general manager Branch Rickey who, at the time, was with the Pirates. Traditionally, baseball players wore their cloth caps at all times when on the field. In the early 1950's Rickey wanted a protective helmet created and asked Muse to develop one. Charlie worked with an inventor and designer and they went through numerous creations before coming up with a helmet that would give maximum protection above the ears, the most vulnerable area for hitters. The Pirates became the first team to wear the helmet in 1952. At first, players called them miner's helmets and said that only sissies would wear them. Two years later a player for the Braves was knocked unconscious for 15 minutes even while wearing a helmet. He said he believed it saved him from serious injury. The next day the Brooklyn Dodgers ordered every player in their organization to wear a batting helmet and the rest of baseball soon followed.

First World Cup Goal

It is the most followed and watched sporting event in the world. Every four years one country's soccer team walks away with the esteemed World Cup. The inaugural cup was held in Montevideo, Uruguay in 1930. It was wintertime and snowing for France's opening match against Mexico. **Lucien Laurent** was standing on the edge of the penalty box and struck home the first World Cup goal in history with the sweep of his right foot. It was a contest that France would go on to win, 4-1. Lucien was the only surviving member of the 1930 team that lived to see France win the World Cup on their home soil in 1998.

Changed the Direction of College Sports

In his first twenty years at the University of Michigan **Don Canham** served as the track coach. He stepped up to the position of athletic director in 1968 and for the next twenty years revolutionized the marketing of college athletics. After the '68 season Don hired an unknown football coach who turned the team into a national power. For years the 101,000 seat stadium averaged 74,000 fans a game. The stadium began to sell out in 1975 and has now sold out 186 consecutive home football games. He broke the mold for athletic directors with his strong marketing techniques. The industry tended to be led by former athletes whose primary qualification was the ability to slap the backs of other athletic directors with the responsibility to primarily hire coaches and schedule opposing teams. During his reign, the University of Michigan won 72 Big Ten championships and made the university's trademark "M" one of the best known symbols in sports. He launched the first major direct mail and advertising campaigns to sell tickets, established fund raising clubs and created income through licensing and marketing souvenirs.

First Latin All-Star

Chico Carrasquel was not the first Latino to play in a major league baseball game—he was the third player to do so. But in 1951 he started at shortstop for the American League in the All-Star game as a member of the Chicago White Sox and singled in his first at bat. With that appearance he became the first Latino to appear in an All-Star game. In all, Chico would play in the All-Star game four times, all with the White Sox. He played in the major leagues from 1950 to 1959 and had a 24 game hitting streak as a rookie. After his retirement, Chico spent several seasons doing Spanish language telecasts of White Sox games.

First Superstar in the NBA

The accomplishments seem to be endless. Selected as one of the 50 greatest players in NBA history and voted the greatest player of the first half of the 20th century. Twice named college player of the year and a three-time All-American. As a pro he led his teams to seven league championships in nine years and three times was the NBA's scoring leader. It was his prowess that forced the NBA to double the width of the "key" underneath the basket and introduce the 24-second clock because teams did not want to turn the ball over to him. **George Mikan** naturally became a member of the first group inducted into the Naismith Basketball Hall of Fame in 1959. After his playing days ended, George became the first commissioner of the American Basketball Association in 1967 and introduced the telegenic red, white and blue basketball.

Popularized Surfing

Dale Velzy started hopping on surfboards at a very young age and had his own board by the time he was 8. Using his grandfather's woodworking tools, Dale began to create his own boards with the help of his father. He started commercially repairing and reshaping boards in 1949 and by 1960 he was running five stores and two factories and selling up to 200 boards a week. At the time he was considered to be the world's largest surfboard manufacturer. His most famous board, the "Pig", debuted in 1955 and is now considered a collectors item. Dale would adapt his technique as boards changed from wood to polyurethane foam and from long to short and back again. Velzyland, a popular surfing spot on Oahu's legendary North Shore is named for him. In 2000, the Doheny Surfing Association named its annual surfing contest in his honor.

Beach Volleyball

He was called the "Godfather of Beach Volleyball" and ran the Manhattan, California Beach Open for decades. It began as a two-man tournament in 1965 and is now a well-regarded contest. **Charlie Saikley** was known worldwide for organizing beach volleyball tournaments. He was also tournament director for Manhattan, CA's annual six-man volleyball tournament that is part of the International Surf Festival. In 1964 Charlie started what is believed to be the first city organized volleyball instruction program in Southern California.

The Slap Shot

Sportswriters of the day called them the 'Bread Line', three players who skated on the same line with the New York Rangers team that won the Stanley Cup in 1940. Left wing **Alex Shibicky** and his two teammates got the name because they were considered the bread and butter of the unit. As a young player with the Rangers in 1935, he would watch his teammate, in practice, use a revolutionary slap shot, an explosive shot with a short backswing. Two years later Alex became the first player to use it in a game. The slapshot would eventually develop into a mainstay in hockey and be recognized as the most dynamic offensive move in the sport.

Harness Racer

At the peak of its popularity, harness racing could draw one-day crowds of 50,000. **Stanley Dancer** dropped out of school in the eighth grade in the 1940's and borrowed $200 from his parents to buy his first horse. Over the next 50 years the numbers would speak for themselves as a trainer, rider owner and breeder: he trained 3 horses to Triple Crown victories, rode winners in 23 Triple Crown races, won 7 horse of the year titles and ranked in the top ten for wins and purses for 20 consecutive years. While not winning races he suffered 32 racing falls, four car accidents, a helicopter crash, a plane crash, two heart attacks and a broken back. Stanley was inducted into the Harness Racing Hall of Fame in 1969.

The Voice of Sports

His was a career of firsts: the first sportscaster to cover the Masters golf tournament, the first to broadcast a college football game coast to coast, the first to serve as a live sports anchor from the Olympics. For six decades **Chris Schenkel** was one of the lead voices of football, basketball, boxing, golf, horse racing, the Olympics and bowling. He was known for his standard comment before going to a commercial, "college football, what a way to spend an autumn afternoon", during his big college game of the week broadcasts. Chris was inducted into 16 halls of fame including the National Sportscasters and Sportswriters and College and Pro Football halls. In 1993 he was given an Emmy for lifetime achievement.

African-American Umpire

His wife said he called it the 'game from hell' because it went on for so long. Despite the length, it was a landmark World Series event as **Charlie Williams** became the first African-American to umpire a World Series game. It was the second longest in Series history at 4 hours and 14 minutes when the Blue Jays beat the Phillies 15-14 in Game 3 of the 1993 Fall Classic. Charlie attended umpire school while he worked the night shift at a factory. After spending time working in the minor leagues he reached the major leagues in 1982. He would say that when the crowd booed he knew he must have done something right. Among the other highlights of his career were working two All-Star games and two championship series in the National League.

TECHNOLOGY

The Einstein of Manned Space Flight

When he was a child **Maxime Faget** and his brother built model submarines using rubber band motors that could submerge and resurface on their own. Maxime joined a select group of 35 scientists in 1958 that formed a special task group to jump-start the newly forming space program. He became an expert in developing a blunt nose cone for the space capsule to ward off the heat it would encounter on its reentry into the earth's atmosphere. His philosophy was "keep it simple" He was an integral part of NASA's team that worked on the Mercury, Gemini and Apollo programs. Even before Neil Armstrong set foot on the moon, Maxime had moved on to join the project that would develop the space shuttle.

Long Lasting Batteries

He took special pride during the Christmas season as people would rush to buy batteries to power the numerous portable devices that require his invention. In 1955 **Lewis Urry** was transferred within National Carbon to improve on the carbon zinc batteries that did not last very long. He took a version of the alkaline battery that Thomas Edison had invented at the turn of the 20th century and converted it to practical use. Lewis' first demonstration of the new alkaline battery took place when he raced two model cars for the company's vice president as his alkaline powered car far outlasted the car running on a D-cell battery. The first alkaline batteries were put on the market in 1959 and renamed the Energizer in 1980. Lewis held 51 patents including one for the lithium battery that is used in cell phones and cameras. Today, an estimated 80% of dry cell batteries worldwide are based on his work. In 1999 he was inducted into the hall of fame at the Smithsonian Institute. His first prototype battery was put on display in the same room as Edison's light bulb.

Fastest Man Alive

He went to watch a flying circus when he was 8 and became fascinated with the show's barnstorming pilot. **Frank Everest** would later earn the nickname 'Speedy

Pete' for the numerous aircraft he would fly on test runs. He flew, for the Air Force, over 15 models of the United States' most advanced planes and rockets and was called the 'fastest man alive' in 1956 when he reached 1,900 miles per hour in a Bell test plane. In 1991 Frank was inducted into the Aerospace Walk of Fame and was honored with a six-foot granite monument. He is also a member of the National Aviation Hall of Fame.

Artificial Vision

At 13, **William Dobelle** was granted a patent for an improvement to an artificial hip. The next year he won the National Science Fair for his homemade X-Ray machine. By 1983 he had turned his direction to the commercial application of artificial implants and the development of vision devices. The Dobelle Artificial Vision System uses a miniature camera that is attached to glasses worn by a blind person. The images are sent to a portable computer that resends them to electrodes fixed to the brain. William said the intention is to improve the mobility of the blind. His other research included artificial hearing for the deaf. He was inducted into the National Academy of Science in 1996 and was nominated for the Nobel Prize in Medicine in 2003.

Hang Gliding

They called him "The Birdman". He was once a professional water-skier who was ranked eighth in the world. In the early 1960's **Bill Bennett** began experimenting with flat kites to lift him off the water. He began using a foldable wing designed by a NASA engineer for spacecraft reentry. Bill modified the wing into his own concept of a glider and began to sell them. In 1969 he glided around the Statue of Liberty on July 4 and landed at its base. Bill popularized the fledgling sport and was the first to accomplish such feats as the first person to fly higher than a mile, flying more than 200 miles under tow, flying a motorized hang glider and building and flying a propeller driven glider. He set a world record reaching 10,000 feet as the first person to launch a hang glider by a hot air balloon. He played the hang gliding stunt double for agent 007 in the 1973 James Bond film 'Live and Let Die' and made the world's highest and longest unassisted free flight when he traveled over 6 miles down into the floor of Death Valley. Several of Bill's gliders are on display at the Smithsonian's Air and Space Museum. He was inducted into the Soaring Hall of Fame and NASA's Space and Technology Hall of Fame.

Jet Innovator

As World War II drew to a close **George Schairer** was with a team of scientists traveling through Germany looking for technical information in abandoned research sites. He found wind tunnel documents that showed planes could be built with "swept back" wings and used with a jet engine. Swept wings prevented the development of shock waves that affected the newly developed jet planes as they approached the speed of sound. George and his team at Boeing were the first to incorporate this new technology. The team also was responsible for putting jet engines in pods beneath the wing that prevents the engine from overheating. In 1957 George received the Daniel Guggenheim Medal which is considered to be aviation's equivalent of the Nobel Prize. Past winners include Orville Wright and Charles Lindbergh.

Open Source Software

In the 1960's the software for simulating the behavior of integrated circuits was slow and unreliable. Designers of chips need to know how the chips will behave before they are manufactured. During this time **Donald Pederson** convinced the University of California at Berkeley to establish a lab to fabricate microchips and allow the students to have a hands on experience to keep pace with the industry. In 1972 he created a fast and accurate program called Spice that became an industry standard. Versions of the code are used today to test chips in computers, cell phones, home appliances and cars. Donald insisted on making the code available to other engineers provided they would notify him of improvements they made and agreed not to sell it for profit. This practice was one of the first to adopt what is commonly known today as open source software.

Lester Machine

It took him only ten weeks to build it in 1935. Today it still remains one of the two primary methods to produce plastic products. **William Lester** created what became known as the Lester machine by developing a process that injected melted plastic into a cavity that resembled a waffle maker. Other machines in use could take six minutes to create a mold, but Bill's took six seconds. With the onset of World War II his innovation became critical to the war effort and brought plastics to the forefront of manufacturing. Today, one-third of all plastics by weight use his method. Bill was inducted into the Plastics Hall of Fame in 1986.

European Space Program

He was admired by the international scientific community for his ability to combine technical success with political effectiveness. **Hubert Curien** was known in France as the father of the European space program. In the 1970's he was alarmed at the failure of the British-led rocket program and the prospect that the US and the Soviet Union would have a complete monopoly in developing the space industry. He persuaded his government to support establishing the Ariane rocket which today now has a dominant role in launching the world's commercial satellites.

Macintosh Computer

He was employee No. 31 in 1978 at Apple Computer before the launch of the Macintosh, iMac, iPod and other products that have since made the company well known. **Jef Raskin wanted** to build an affordable computer designed for nontechnology consumers, a novel idea at a time when using a computer required memorizing complex codes and commands. He oversaw the development of a computer he named the Macintosh, after his favorite kind of apple. Jef is considered to be responsible for its drag and drop feature and the icons and windows on the computer screen. Jef left Apple two years before the Macintosh was released for sale to the public in 1984.

Remote Sensing

For five decades **Robert Colwell** taught at the University of California at Berkeley. He acquired an interest in aerial photography during World War II when he interpreted photographs in the South Pacific and taught others to do the same for navy intelligence. At Berkeley he utilized his knowledge to adapt the techniques to forestry, mapmaking, land planning and agriculture. In the 1960's Robert was able to accumulate vast amounts of biological data and, as a result, diseases in crops, moisture levels in soil and insect infestations in orchards and forests were detected. In the 1970's he became an advisor for a project in Brazil in which scientists there used satellite radar to map a large area of the Amazon basin.

Alternative Fuel Vehicles

She was the first woman chosen as a fellow by the Society of Automotive Engineers. Growing up, **Roberta Nichols** followed her father to junkyards. She learned to weld and worked with him on his vintage cars. She would not get a college degree until age 37 due her commitments to raising a family and would eventually earn a doctorate. Roberta was hired by the Ford car company in 1979 and led the development of their alternative fuel vehicles. She worked extensively on methanol, ethanol, natural gas and electric vehicles and began experimenting with hybrid electric and gasoline cars. In 1994 she finished second racing Ford's electric van in a 600 mile electric and solar vehicle road rally, the world's largest.

Audiologist

While working for the National Institute of Standards and Technology, **E. Harris Nober** tested the volume of smoke detectors and the time it took for people who were sleeping to get up and leave. The study's results were used to determine the noise levels for residential smoke detectors. In the 1980's he developed a system of flashing strobe lights that would alert the hearing impaired. The frequency of the flashes would alert them to whether the doorbell or the telephone was ringing or the smoke detector had gone off. There was no system prior to his work and many tragedies going forward were avoided. He received a Distinguished Career Achievement Award from the American Academy of Audiology in 1998.

Rocket Carriers

In the early 1960's the US space program was on a fast track toward manned spaceflights to the moon. NASA faced the problem of moving large rockets from the storage facility to their launching pads at Cape Canaveral, Florida. They decided on a crawler concept, a four-track vehicle that could carry as much as 12 million pounds. **Donald Buchanan** directed the design and development of the crawler that was able to haul both rockets and mobile launchers for several miles. A second crawler was also built, and the two 131-foot-long vehicles were later used in launching the Skylab space stations and are still essential in preparing for flights of the space shuttle. In addition, Don designed three mobile launchers that were used in the Saturn 5 missions to the moon. Each was 363 feet tall. He was awarded NASA's Distinguished Service Medal in 1974.

The Integrated Circuit

When a severe ice storm took down the phone lines in rural Kansas, **Jack Kilby**'s father worked with amateur radio operators to communicate with the customers of his small power company. That incident sparked Jack's interest in electronics and paved the path for his invention in later years that would transform the world. In 1958 Jack was working alone at a Texas Instruments lab in Dallas and created the first integrated circuit prototype. It yielded a thin chip of crystal connecting previously separate components like transistors, resistors and capacitors into a single device. It gave rise to the information age and resulted in an explosion of consumer products such as music and media players, digital cameras, cell phones, calculators, computers and video games. Jack earned more than 60 patents and also invented the hand-held calculator. He received the Nobel Prize in Physics in 2000, won the National Medal of Science and was inducted into the National Inventors Hall of Fame.

Music Synthesizer

He did not invent it, RCA did in 1955. But their synthesizer was a primitive version that was the size of a room and whose sounds were controlled by punching holes in tape. **Robert Moog** added a keyboard and did for the instrument what Les Paul and Leo Fender had done for the guitar. Its portability enabled musicians to bring it into the concert hall and the sound was easy to manipulate. In 1964, Robert's synthesizer sold for $11,000 while RCA's went for $100,000. College music schools started electronic music labs built around his instrument. Rock groups including the Beatles used his sound on their records. By the early 1970's the use of the Moog synthesizer was everywhere. His name became so closely associated with electronic sound that that it was often used, incorrectly, to describe synthesizers of all kinds. In 2001, Robert was awarded the Polar Prize by the King of Sweden for his contributions to music.

The Laser

They are an essential part of daily living and are found in such items as DVD players and bar code scanners. Various forms of the laser can be used for communications, surgery and precise measurements of the distance between the Earth and the Moon. **Gordon Gould** sketched some ideas on his thoughts for the development of the laser during the same period in the late 1950's that others were also involved in its creation. He envisioned a device that would be used for welding, cutting and heating and would do for optics what transistors had done for electronics. Gordon is created with coining the acronym 'laser' from the mouthful—light amplitude for stimulating the emission of radiation. He was inducted into the National Inventors Hall of Fame in 1991.

Honor Roll

	Born	Died	Age
Ruth Adams	Los Angeles	La Jolla, CA	81
John Addington	India	Great Britain	90
Keiiti Aki	Yokohoma, Japan	Reunion Island	75
Samuel Alderson	Cleveland, OH	Los Angeles	90
Sharifa Alkhateeb	Philadelphia, PA	Ashburn, VA	58
Thomas B. Allen	Nashville, TN	Sarasota, FL	76
Mansour Armaly	Shefa Amr, Palestine	Washington, DC	78
Al Aronowitz	Bordentown, NJ	Elizabeth, NJ	77
George Atkinson	Shanghai, China	Los Angeles	69
Bobby Avila	Veracruz, Mexico	Veracruz, Mexico	78
Julius Axelrod	New York City	Rockville, MD	92
John Bahcall	Shreveport, LA	New York City	70
William Bailey	Syracuse, NY	New York City	78
John Baldry	Haddon, England	Vancouver, Canada	64
Ernesta Ballard	Philadelphia, PA	Philadelphia, PA	85
Alexander Bassin	New York City	Tallahassee, FL	92
Fereydoon B.	Iran	Fairfax, VA	73
Joe Belden	Eagle Pass, TX	Washington, DC	90
Peter Beneson	London	Oxford, England	83
Harold Benjamin	Philadelphia, PA	Marina del Rey, CA	80
Bill Bennett	Korumburra, Australia	Lake Havasu, AZ	73
Hans Bethe	Strasbourg, Germany	Ithaca, NY	98

	Born	*Died*	*Age*
Keter Betts	Port Chester, NY	Silver Spring, MD	77
Wilfred Bigelow	Brandon, Canada	Toronto, Canada	91
Joseph Bogen	Cincinnati, OH	Pasadena, CA	78
Bruce Bolt	New S. Wales, Australia	Oakland, CA	75
Alain Bombard	Paris	Toulon, France	80
Gerard Bond	Altus. OK	New York City	65
F. C. Branch	Hamlet, NC	Philadelphia, PA	82
Ure Bronfenbrenner	Moscow	Ithaca, NY	88
Gwydion Brooke	Newmarket, England	England	93
Herbert Brown	London, England	West Lafayette, IN	92
Richard Brown	New York City	Hunting. Beach, CA	64
Tulley Brown	Los Angeles, CA	La Crescenta, CA	72
Donald Buchanan	Macon, GA	Titusville, FL	82
John Buck	Hartford, CT	Sykesville, MD	92
Sonja Buckley	Zurich, Switzerland	Baltimore, MD	86
Ray Budde	St. Louis, MO	Springfield, MA	82
David Bushnell	St. Paul, MN	Laguna Beach, CA	91
George Campbell	Dingwall, Scotland	Brigthton, England	92
Laura Canales	Kingsville, TX	Corpus Christi, TX	50
Don Canham	Oak Park, IL	Saline, MI	87
Chico Carrasquel	Caracas, Venezuela	Caracas, Venezuela	77
Sidney Carter	Boston, MA	Mashpee, MA	92
Paul Cassidy	Cherry Valley, IL	Milwaukee, WI	94
Homer Chapman	Darlington, WI	Irvine, CA	106
Shiing-Shen Chern	Jiaxing, China	Tianjin, China	93
Kenneth Clark	Panama Canal Zone	Hastings, NY	90
Paul Clayton	Salt Lake City, UT	Draper, UT	91

	Born	Died	Age
Helen Claytor	Minneapolis, MN	Grand Rapids, MI	98
William Cleland	Sydney, Australia	England	92
Morris Cohen	Chelsea, MA	Swampscott, MA	93
Robert Colwell	Star, ID	Walnut Creek, CA	87
Thomas Concannon	New York City	New York City	61
Robert Creeley	Arlington, MA	Odessa, TX	78
William Crosby	Wheeling, WVA	Joplin, MO	90
George Crikelair	Green Bay, WI	Ft. Lauderdale, FL	84
Hubert Curien	Cornimont, France	France	80
John Dacie	London	London	92
H. David Dalquist	Minneapolis, MN	Edina, MN	86
Stanley Dancer	West Windsor, NJ	Pompano Beach, FL	78
Mary Dann	Eureka County, NV	Crescent Valley, NV	80
George Dantzig	Portland, OR	Palo Alto, CA	90
Horace Davenport	Philadelphia, PA	Ann Arbor, MI	92
Glenn Davis	Claremont, CA	La Quinta, CA	80
Gerard Debreu	Calais, France	Paris, France	83
Clarence Dennis	St. Paul, MN	St. Paul, MN	96
Martin Denny	New York City	Honolulu, HI	93
Uli Derickson	Czechoslovakia	Tucson, AZ	60
Jacques Derrida	El-Biar, Algeria	Paris, France	74
Timothy Diener	Elizabeth, NJ	Napa, CA	94
Nanna Ditzel	Copenhagen, Denmark	Copenhagen	81
William Dobelle	Pittsfield, MA	New York City	62
Richard Doll	Hampton, England	Oxford, England	92
Thomas Donahue	Healdton, OK	Ann Arbor, MI	83
Albert Dorskind	New York City	Los Angeles, CA	82

	Born	*Died*	*Age*
Otis Duncan	Nocona, TX	Santa Barbara, CA	82
Alan Dundes	New York City	Berkeley, CA	70
John Ebstein	Stettin, Germany	Palm Beach, FL	92
Isidore Edelman	New York City	New York City	84
Simon Eisdorfer	New York City	Manhasset, NY	87
Will Eisner	New York City	Ft. Lauderdale, FL	87
Frank Everest	Fairmont, WVA	Tucson, AZ	84
Maxime Faget	Stann Creek, Belize	Clear Lake, TX	83
Frederick Fennell	Cleveland, OH	Siesta Key, FL	90
M. Irene Ferrer	Elberon, NJ	New York City	89
Fred Fisher	St. Louis, MO	Inverness Park, CA	68
Arthur Fletcher	Camp Huachuca, AZ	Washington, DC	80
Vincent Fontana	New York City	Block Island, RI	81
John Ford, Jr.	Hollywood, CA	Scottsdale, AZ	81
James Forman	Chicago, IL	Washington, DC	76
Peter Foy	London	Las Vegas	79
Andre Frank	Berlin, Germany	Luxembourg	76
F. K. Freas	Hornell, NY	Los Angeles	82
Lawrence Freedman	Gardner, MA	Chicago, IL	85
E. D. Freis	Chicago, IL	Washington, DC	92
John Gaines	Sherburne, NY	Lexington, KY	76
J. Donald M. Gass	Prince Edward Island	Nashville, TN	76
Prentice Gautt	Oklahoma City, OK	Lawrence, KS	67
H. Bentley Glass	Yehsien, China	Boulder, CO	98
Isabelle Goldenson	New York City	Sarasota, FL	84
Sidney Goldring	Poland	Chesterfield, MO	81
Milton Gordon	St. Paul, MN	Seattle, WA	75

	Born	**Died**	**Age**
Gordon Gould	New York City	New York City	85
Joe Grant	New York City	Glendale, CA	96
Samuel Gravely	Richmond, VA	Haymarket, VA	82
Howard Gruber	New York City	New York City	82
Lalo Guerrero	Tucson, Arizona	Palm Springs, CA	88
Horace Hagedorn	New York City	Sands Point, NY	89
Elizabeth Hall	New York City	Canaan, CT	95
Mary Hallaren	Lowell, MA	McLean, VA	97
Frank Harary	New York City	Las Cruces, NM	83
Murray Harper	Glasgow, Scotland	Scotland	72
Paul Harper	Chicago	Evanston, IL	89
Allen Haskell	New Beford, MA	New Bedford, MA	69
James Haskins	Demopolis, AL	New York City	63
Mike Hearn	Kent, England	Namibia	32
Anderl Heckmair	Munich, Germany	Germany	98
Harry Heltzer	Cincinnati, OH	Lenoir, NC	94
Maurice Hilleman	Miles City, MT	Philadelphia, PA	85
Carlos Hormaeche	Montevideo. Uruguay	Uruguay	64
Norman Horowitz	Pittsburgh, PA	Pasadena, CA	90
Rollin Hotchkiss	South Britain, CT	Lenox, MA	93
James Houston	Toronto	Stonington, CT	83
Ruth Huenemann	Waukon, IA	Oakland, CA	95
Bob Hunter	Winnipeg, Manitoba	Toronto	63
George Isaak	Pilica, Poland	England	72
Sue Jackson	Glossop, England	England	59
Fred Joerger	Pekin, IL	Woodland Hills, CA	91
Mary Kim Joh	Seoul, Korea	New York City	101

	Born	*Died*	*Age*
John Johnson	Arkansas City, AR	Chicago	87
Philip Johnson	Cleveland, OH	New Canaan,CT	98
Georgeanna Jones	Baltimore, MD	Norfolk, VA	92
J. Calvin Jureit	Baltimore, MD	Stuart, FL	87
Jasper Kane	New York City	Boca Raton, FL	101
Bob Karstens	Davenport, IA	Redlands, CA	89
Robert Kearns	Gary, IN	Sykesville, MD	77
Charles Keeling	Scranton, PA	Hamilton, MT	77
Paul Keene	Lititz, PA	Mechanicsburg, PA	94
Leonid Khachiyan	St. Petersburg, Russia	S. Brunswick, NJ	52
Jack Kilby	Jefferson City, MO	Dallas, TX	81
Manfred Korfmann	Cologne, German	Tubingen, Germany	63
S. J. Korsmeyer	Beardstown, IL	Boston, MA	54
Christina Korten	Santa Monica, CA	Los Angeles	55
Bobby Kramer	Prairie County, MT	Billings, MT	91
Margot Kruskall	New York City	Dover, MA	56
John La Montagne	Mexico City, Mexico	Mexico City, Mexico	61
Paul Lacy	Trinway, OH	Zanesville, OH	81
Philip Lamantia	San Francisco	San Francisco	77
Harry Lampert	New York City	Boca Raton, FL	88
Frances Langford	Lakeland, FL	Jensen Beach, FL	92
Marc Lappe	Irvington, NJ	Gualala, CA	62
Katherine Lathrop	Lawton, OK	Las Cruces, NM	89
John Laughlin	Canton, MO	New York City	86
Lucien Laurent	France	Besancon, France	90
Ernest Lehman	New York City	Los Angeles	89
James Lebron	New York City	West Islip, NY	76

	Born	Died	Age
Naomi Leff	New York City	New York City	66
William Lester	New York City	Delray Beach, FL	97
Karl Linn	Dessow, Germany	Berkley, CA	81
W. B. Lipes	Newcastle, VA	New Bern, NC	84
Terry Lipton	Chicago, IL	Los Angeles	66
J. William Littler	Manilus, NY	Providence, RI	89
Sol Londe	St. Louis, MO	Reseda, CA	100
Arthur Lydiard	Auckland, New Zealand	Houston, TX	87
Saunders Mac Lane	Norwich, CT	San Francisco	95
Jackson Mac Low	Chicago, IL	New York City	82
Maclyn McCarty	South Bend, IN	New York City	93
Nellie McCaslin	Cleveland, OH	New York City	90
Shannon McGowan	Los Angeles, CA	Point Richmond, CA	61
Noel Mander	Crouch, England	London	93
Cindy Marano	Philadelphia, PA	San Francisco	57
Sheldon Margen	Chicago, IL	Berkeley, CA	85
Jacob Marinksy	Buffalo, NY	Buffalo, NY	87
Alicia Markova	London	Bath England	94
Alex. Marshack	New York City	New York City	86
Jay Marshall	Abington, MA	Chicago	85
Jimmy Martin	Sneedville, TN	Nashville, TN	71
Ernst Mayer	Kempten, Germany	Bedford, MA	100
Linda Maurer	Turlock, CA	Turlock, CA	65
Phyllis Meadow	Boston, MA	New York City	80
Betty Melville	Baltimore, MD	Baltimore, MD	78
Rinus Michels	Amsterdam	Aalst, Belgium	77
George Mikan	Joliet, IL	Scottsdale, AZ	80

	Born	*Died*	*Age*
George Molchan	Hobart, IN	Hobart, IN	82
Nell Mondy	Pochahontas, AR	Ithaca, NY	83
Robert Moog	New York City	Asheville, NC	71
Constance Motley	New Haven, CT	New York City	84
Jack Munushian	Rochester, NY	Los Angeles	81
Lyle Murphy	Berlin, Germany	Los Angeles	96
Charlie Muse	United States	Sun City Center, FL	87
Gaylord Nelson	Clear Lake, WI	Kensington, MD	89
Norman Newell	Chicago, IL	Leonia, NJ	96
Jack Nichols	Washington, DC	Coca Beach, FL	67
Roberta Nichols	Santa Monica, CA	Plymouth, MI	73
E. Harris Nober	New York City	Arlington, VA	77
Anne Noggle	Evanston, IL	Albuquerque, NM	83
Memphis Norman	Monroeville, AL	Falls Church, VA	62
Alvin Novick	New York City	New Haven, CT	79
K. Patrick Okura	Los Angeles	Bethesda, MD	93
Jean O'Leary	Kingston, NY	San Clemente, CA	57
John Ostrom	New York City	Litchfield, CT	77
Zoltan Ovary	Kolozsvar, Hungary	New York City	98
Ellis Page	San Diego	McLean, VA	81
Christopher Pallis	Bombay, India	Great Britain	81
Eduardo Paolozzi	Leith, England	England	81
Toni Parker	Winston-Salem, NC	Stamford, CT	58
Benjamin Paul	New York City	Atlanta, GA	94
Ruth Pease	Ashland, NE	Los Angeles	96
Donald Pederson	Hallock, MN	Concord, CA	79
Charles Pereira	London, England	England	91

	Born	Died	Age
Elwood Perry	Hickory, NC	Taylorsville, NC	90
Paul Perry	Camden, NJ	Princeton, NJ	95
Hy Peskin	New York City	Herzliya, Israel	89
Jeanne Petrek	Youngstown, OH	New York City	57
Helen Phillips	St. Louis, MO	New York City	85
Hugh Phillips	London	London	65
Melba Phillips	Hazleton, IN	Petersburg, IN	97
Larry Ponza	Glenwood, CA	Santa Cruz, CA	86
Jef Raskin	New York City	Pacifica, CA	61
Derek Ratcliffe	London	Arctic Circle	75
Charles ReVelle	Rochester, NY	Baltimore, MD	67
Paul Ricoeur	Valence, France	Chatenay, France	92
Jon Riffel	Arkansas	Pacific Palisades, CA	84
Arthur Robinson	Montreal, Canada	Madison, WI	89
Ruth Roemer	Hartford, CT	Los Angeles	89
Tom Rogers	Minneapolis, MN	Charlottesville, VA	87
Joseph Rotblat	Warsaw, Poland	London	96
Miriam Rothschild	Ashton, England	Ashton, England	96
Stanley Sadie	London, England	Cossington, England	74
Charlie Saikley	Terre Haute, IN	Manhat. Beach, CA	69
Herb Sargent	Philadelphia, PA	New York City	81
Cicely Saunders	London	London	87
Paul Sawyer	Norfolk, VA	Richmond, VA	88
George Schairer	Wilkinsburg, PA	Kenmore, WA	91
Edward Schantz	Hartford, WI	Madison, WI	96
Albert Schatz	Norwich, CT	Philadelphia, PA	84
Chris Schenkel	Bippus, IN	Fort Wayne, IN	82

	Born	*Died*	*Age*
Bob Schiffer	Seattle, WA	Los Angeles	88
Miriam Schlein	New York City	New York City	78
Ronald Scott	London	Altadena, CA	76
Gordon Shaw	Atlantic City, NJ	Laguna Beach, CA	72
Alex Shibicky	Winnipeg, Canada	S. Surrey, Canada	91
William Silverman	Cleveland, OH	Greenbrae, CA	87
Harry Simeone	Newark, NJ	New York City	94
Morris Simon	Johannesburg	Boston, MA	79
James Simmons	Philadelphia, PA	Encino, CA	79
Czeslaw Slania	Czeladz, Poland	Krakow, Poland	83
Robert Slutzky	New York City	Abington, PA	75
Joseph Smagorinsky	New York City	Skillman, NJ	81
Edward Smith	St. Louis, MO	Culver City, CA	81
Leslie Smith	Enfield, England	London	87
Lynn Smith	Minnesota	Minneapolis, MN	84
Jimmy Smith	Norristown, PA	Phoenix, AZ	76
Humphrey Spender	London	Ulting, England	94
Philip Spaulding	Snoqualmie Valley, WA	Magnolia, WA	92
Julian Stanley	East Point, GA	Columbia, MD	87
Eugene Stead	Atlanta, GA	Bullock, NC	96
Brandt Steele	Indianapolis, IN	Denver, CO	97
Sara Stein	New York City	Vinalhaven, ME	69
Leo Sternbach	Croatia	Chapel Hill, NC	97
Harold Stevenson	Dines, WY	Ann Arbor, MI	80
Peter Stokes	Haddonfield, NJ	New York City	78
Jeremy Swan	Sligo, Ireland	Los Angeles	82
Kenzo Tange	Osaka, Japan	Tokyo	91

	Born	*Died*	*Age*
Lauriston Taylor	New York City	Mitchellville, MD	102
William Taylor	Portland, OR	Washington, DC	62
Esther Thelen	New York City	Bloomington, IN	63
Gerry Thomas	Seward. NE	Phoenix, AZ	83
H. Tomaszewski	Warsaw, Poland	Warsaw, Poland	91
Jackie Torrence	Chicago, IL	Salisbury, NC	60
Andrew Toti	Visalia, CA	Modesto, CA	89
William Trager	Newark, NJ	New York City	94
Lewis Urry	Pontypool, Ontario	Middleburg, OH	77
John Vane	Worcestershire, England	Farnborough, Eng.	77
John Vaughan	Merthyr Tydfil, England	London	79
Consuelo Velazquez	Ciudad Guzman, Mexico	Mexico City	88
Dale Velzy	Hermosa Beach, CA	Mission Viejo, CA	77
Avabai Wadia	Sri Lanka	London	91
George Walker	London	England	78
Mary Washington	Vicksburg, MS	Chicago	99
Sidney Waxman	Providence, RI	Storrs, CT	81
Brenda Weathers	Smithfield, TX	Long Beach, CA	68
Dick Weber	Indianapolis, IN	Florissant, MO	75
Joseph Weiss	Cincinnati, OH	San Francisco, CA	80
Sy Wexler	New York City	Los Angeles	88
John White	Waukegan, IL	Virginia, Beach, VA	87
Sheldon White	New York City	Boston, MA	76
Charlie Williams	Denver, CO	Oak Lawn, IL	61
Anthony Williamson	New York City	St. John's, Canada	69
Victor Wouk	New York City	New York City	86
Cara Yates	Chicago, IL	Sutton, MA	34

	Born	*Died*	*Age*
Akira Yoshizawa	Kaminokawa, Japan	Ogikubo, Japan	94
Morris Ziff	New York City	Dallas, TX	91
John Ziman	New Zealand	England	79

Sources

I relied on The New York Times, Los Angeles Times, the Guardian and the Daily Telegraph, both of London, as my primary resources. These newspapers formed the basis of my research and I have drawn extensively from each of them. I used the Internet newspaper edition of the below sources as well as websites that offered additional material.

Newspaper Abbreviations:

NYT: The New York Times
LAT: Los Angles Times
G: Guardian
T: Daily Telegraph
WP: The Washington Post
AP: Associated Press

Ruth Adams: LAT, NYT
Lord Addington: T
Keiiti Aki: LAT, NYT
Samuel Alderson: NYT, LAT, AP
Sharifa Alkhateeb: NYT, LAT
Thomas B. Allen: NYT
Mansour Armaly: WP, NYT
Al Aronowitz: NYT, LAT
George Atkinson: LAT, NYT
Bobby Avila: LAT, NYT
Julius Axelrod: NYT, LAT
John Bahcall: NYT, LAT, T
William Bailey: NYT
John Baldry: G, T, NYT
Ernesta Ballard: Philadelphia Inquirer, Philadelphia Daily News, NYT

Alexander Bassin: NYT, daytop.org
Fereydoon Batmanghelidj: WP, LAT
Joe Belden: NYT, LAT
Harold Benjamin: LAT, medicalnewstoday.com
Peter Benenson: G, T, NYT, LAT
Bill Bennett: LAT. NYT, T
Hans Bethe: NYT, LAT
Keter Betts: WP, NYT
Wilfred Bigelow: NYT, LAT
Joseph Bogen: LAT
Bruce Bolt: San Francisco Chronicle, LAT, NYT
Alain Bombard: NYT, T, London Times
Gerard Bond: NYT, earthinstitute.columbia.edu
Frederick Branch: AP
Ure Bronfenbrenner: NYT, LAT
Gwydion Brooke: G
Herbert Brown: LAT, Lafayette Journal and Courier
Richard Brown: LAT
Tully Brown: LAT
Donald Buchanan: NYT
John Buck: NYT
Sonja Buckley: NYT, LAT
Ray Budde: Boston Globe, NYT
David Bushnell: LAT, NYT
George Campbell: WP, The Scotsman
Laura Canales: WP, AP
Don Canham: Detroit Free Press, The Daily Oakland Press, LAT
Chico Carrasquel: LAT
Sidney Carter: NYT
Paul Cassidy: LAT
Homer Chapman: LAT
Shiing-Shen Chern: NYT
Kenneth Clark: NYT, WP
Paul Clayton: LAT
Helen Claytor: LAT, NYT, ci.grand-rapids.mi.us
William Cleland: G
Morris Cohen: NYT, LAT
Robert Colwell: NYT, berkeley.edu

Thomas Concannon: NYT
Robert Creeley: LAT, NYT
George Crikelair: NYT
William Crosby: NYT
Hubert Curien: T
John Dacie: G, T, London Times
H. David Dalquist: LAT, NYT, nordicware.com
Stanley Dancer: NYT, LAT, AP
Mary Dann: LAT
George Dantzig: LAT, NYT, T
Horace Davenport: NYT, Detroit Free Press
Glenn Davis: LAT, NYT
Gerard Debreu: LAT, berkeley.edu
Clarence Dennis: Minneapolis Star-Tribune, NYT, LAT, med.umn.edu
Martin Denny: LAT, NYT, Honolulu Start–Bulletin, spaceagepop.com
Uli Derickson: NYT, LAT
Jacques Derrida: NYT, WP, T
Timothy Diener: LAT, NYT, AP, stmarys-ca.edu
Nanna Ditzel: AP, G, r20thcentury.com
William Dobelle: Syosset-Jericho Tribune, LAT
Richard Doll: G, T, NYT, LAT
Thomas Donahue: NYT
Albert Dorskind: LAT
Otis Duncan: Santa Barbara News-Press, NYT
Alan Dundes: LAT, NYT, WP, San Francisco Chronicle, G, afsnet.org
John Ebstein: NYT
Isidore Edelman: NYT
Simon Eisdorfer: NYT
Will Eisner: NYT, willeisner.com
Frank Everest: LAT
Maxime Faget: Houston Chronicle, LAT, NYT, WP
Frederick Fennell: WP, G
M. Irene Ferrer: NYT
Fred Fisher: LAT, NYT
Arthur Fletcher: NYT, LAT
Vicent Fontana: NYT
John Ford, Jr.: NYT, LAT
James Forman: WP, NYT

Peter Foy: LAT, NYT, variety.com
Andre Gunder Frank: G
F. K. Freas: NYT,
Lawrence Freedman: Chicago Sun-Times, NYT
E. D. Freis: NYT
John Gaines: Louisville Courier-Journal, bloodhorse.com, AP
J. Donald M. Gass: NYT, The Reporter/Vanderbilt Medical Center
Prentice Gautt: AP
H. Bentley Glass: LAT, NYT
Isabelle Goldenson: NYT, ucp.org
Sidney Goldring: NYT, record.wustl.edu
Milton Gordon: Seattle Post-Intelligencer, AP
Gordon Gould: NYT, WP, AP
Joe Grant: G, LAT, savedisney.com
Samuel Gravely: WP, NYT, LAT
Howard Gruber: NYT, G
Lalo Guerrero: LAT, AP
Horace Hagedorn: NYT, LAT, T
Elizabeth Hall: NYT, simons-rock.edu
Mary Hallaren: WP, NYT
Frank Harary: NYT
Murray Harper: G
Paul Harper: NYT, uchospitals.edu, Chicago Sun-Times
Allen Haskell: NYT
James Haskins: NYT, LAT
Mike Hearn: G, T
Anderl Heckmair: T, LAT
Harry Heltzer: NYT
Maurice Hilleman: NYT, G, T
Carlos Hormaeche: G, ncl.ac.uk
Norman Horowitz: LAT, NYT
Rollin Hotchkiss: Boston Globe, NYT
James Houston: NYT
Ruth Huenemann–San Francisco Chronicle, LAT, berkeley.edu
Bob Hunter: greenpeace.org, AP, G
George Isaak: T
Sue Whitworth-Jackson: G
Fred Joerger: LAT, AP

Mary Kim Joh: NYT
John Johnson: NYT, LAT, G
Philip Johnson: NYT
Georgeanna Jones: Virginian-Pilot, WP, NYT, T
J. Calvin Jureit: Miami Herald, NYT
Jasper Kane: NYT, LAT
Bob Karstens: Redlands Daily Facts, LAT, AP
Robert Kearns: WP, AP
Charles Keeling: LAT, NYT, WP, G, T
Paul Keene: Sunbury Daily Item, WP, LAT
Leonid Khachiyan: NYT
Jack Kilby: LAT, NYT, G, T
Manfred Korfmann: NY, London Times
S. J. Korsmeyer: NYT
Christina Korten: LAT
Bobby Brooks Kramer: Billings Gazette, AP
Margot Kruskall: NYT
John La Montagne: WP, biomedcentral.com, NYT
Paul Lacy: NYT, LAT, Washington University Record
Philip Lamantia: San Francisco Chronicle, LAT, NYT
Harry Lampert: Palm Beach Post, NYT, LAT, WP
Frances Langford: LAT, NYT
Marc Lappe: NYT, LAT, organicconsumers.org
Katherine Lathrop: NYT
John Laughlin: NYT
Lucien Laurent: G, answers.com
James Lebron: NYT
Naomi Leff: NYT, LAT
Ernest Lehman: LAT, NYT
William Lester: NYT, Boston Globe
Wheeler Lipes: NYT, LAT
Terry Lipton: LAT
Karl Linn: NYT,LAT
J.William Littler: NYT
Sol Londe: LAT
Arthur Lydiard: LAT, NYT
Saunders Mac Lane: LAT, T, uchicago.edu
Jackson Mac Low: LAT

Maclyn McCarthy: NYT, LAT
Nellie McCaslin: NYT, nyu.edu
Shannon McGowan: San Francisco Chronicle, LAT
Noel Mander: G, T
Cindy Marano: LAT, WP
Sheldon Margen: LAT, SF Chronicle, Berkeley.edu
Jacob Marinksy: NYT, AP, T
Alicia Markova: NYT, LAT
Alexander Marshack: NYT
Jay Marshall: NYT, New York Sun, magicwebchannel.com
Jimmy Martin: AP, cmt.com, G
Linda Maurer: LAT, AP
Ernst Mayer: NYT, LAT, G, T
Phyllis Meadow: NYT
Betty Leslie-Melvill: NYT, T
Rinus Michels: T, LAT
George Mikan: LAT, NYT
George Molchan: LAT
Nell Mondy: NYT, cornell.edu
Robert Moog: NYT, LAT, T
Constance Baker Motley: NYT, LAT
Jack Munushian: NYT, usc.edu, The Daily Trojan
Lyle Murphy: LAT
Charlie Muse: NYT, LAT
Isao Nakauchi: AP
Gaylord Nelson: WP, NYT
Norman Newell: NYT, ncseweb.org
Jack Nichols: WP, NYT, AP
Roberta Nichols: LAT
E. Harris Nober: NYT
Anne Noggle: LAT, G
Memphis Norman: WP, LAT
Alvin Novick: NYT, yalemedicalgroup.org
K. Patrick Okura: WP, LAT
Jean O'Leary: LAT
John Ostrom: NYT, LAT, T
Zoltan Ovary: NYT
Ellis Page: NYT

Christopher Pallis: G
Eduardo Paolozzi: G, T
Toni Trent Parker: NYT
Benjamin Paul: LAT, NYT
Ruth Pease: LAT, hollywoodschoolhouse.org
Donald Pederson: NYT
Charles Pereira: T
Elwood Perry: NYT, LAT
Paul Perry: NYT, towntopics.com
Hy Peskin: LAT
Jeanne Petrek: NYT, New York Daily News
Helen Phillips: NYT
Hugh Phillips: London Times, G, T
Melba Phillips: NYT, WP, uchicago.edu
Larry Ponza: Santa Cruz Sentinel, AP
Jef Raskin: San Franciso Chronicle, NYT, raskincenter.org, LAT,
businessweek.com
Derek Ratcliffe: G, T
Charles ReVelle: NYT, jhu.edu
Paul Ricoeur: NYT, LAT, G, T
Jon Riffel: LAT
Arthur Robinson, LAT, T
Ruth Roemer: LAT
Tom Rogers: WP
Joseph Rotblat: G, NYT, LAT
Miriam Rothschild: G, London Times, T, NYT
Stanley Sadie: T, G, NYT, LAT
Charlie Saikley: LAT, AP
Herb Sargent: NYT
Cicely Saunders: G, T, LAT
Paul Sawyer: Virginian-Pilot, AP, LAT
George Schairer: Seattle Times, NYT, LAT
Edward Schantz: NYT, T, London Times
Albert Schatz: NYT, G
Chris Schenkel: NYT, LAT
Bob Schiffer: variety.com, vcall.com, G
Miriam Schlein: NYT
Ronald Scott: LAT, caltech.edu

Gordon Shaw: LAT, London Times
Alex Shibicky: NYT, AP, nhl.com,
William Silverman: San Francisco Chronicle, NYT slania.nu
Harry Simeone: LAT, jerryosborne.com
James Simmons: LAT
Morris Simon: NYT
Czeslaw Slania: NYT
Robert Slutzky: NYT
Joseph Smagorinsky: NYT, LAT
Edward Smith: LAT
Leslie Smith: NYT, T, LAT
Lynn Smith: AP
Jimmy Smith: NYT, T
Philip Spaulding: Seattle Times, LAT
Humphrey Spender: G, T, NYT, LAT
Julian Stanley: NYT, jhu.edu
Eugene Stead: NYT, esteadjr.org, dukenews.edu
Brandt Steele: LAT, NYT
Sara Stein: NYT, LAT
Leo Sternbach: NYT, LAT, G, T
Harold Stevenson: NYT, LAT
Peter Stokes: NYT
Jeremy Swan: LAT
Kenzo Tange: LAT, G, T
Lauriston Taylor: NYT
William Taylor: WP
Esther Thelen: LAT, WP
Gerry Thomas: WP, NYT, AP, bbc.co.uk
Henryk Tomaszewski: G, NYT
Jackie Torrence: LAT
Andrew Toti: LAT, NYT
William Trager: NYT, LAT
Lewis Urry: Cleveland Plain Dealer, LAT
John Vane: LAT, T, G
John Vaughan: T
Consuelo Velazquez: NYT
Dale Velzy: LAT, NYT, G, AP
Avabai Wadia: G

George Walker: G, T, London Times, Honolulu Star-Bulletin
Mary Washington: Chicago Defender, accountingweb.com, LAT, NYT
Sidney Waxman: NYT, uconn.edu
Brenda Weathers: LAT, Long Beach Press Telegram
Dick Weber: NYT, bpaa.com
Joseph Weiss: San Francisco Chronicle, LAT, NYT
Sy Wexler: LAT, NYT
John White: NYT
Sheldon White: NYT
Charlie Williams: Chicago Tribune, AP
Anthony Williamson: NYT
Victor Wouk: LAT, NYT
Cara Dunne-Yates: Boston Globe, Chicago Sun-Times, LAT
Akira Yoshizawa: NYT, G
Morris Ziff: Dallas Morning News, NYT
John Ziman: G, T

978-0-595-37762-6
0-595-37762-9